DIXIE'S FORGOTTEN PEOPLE

Minorities in Modern America

Editors

Warren F. Kimball

David Edwin Harrell, Jr.

DIXIE'S FORGOTTEN PEOPLE

THE SOUTH'S POOR WHITES

J. Wayne Flynt

INDIANA UNIVERSITY PRESS
BLOOMINGTON AND LONDON

Manufactured in the United States of America

Library of Congress Cataloging in Publication Data
Flynt, J · Wayne, 1940-
    Dixie's forgotten people.
    (Minorities in modern America series)
    Bibliography: p.
    Includes index.
    1. Poor—Southern States. I. Title. II. Series:
Minorities in modern America.
HC107.A13F66   301.44'1   78-20613
ISBN 0-253-19765-1   cl.
ISBN 0-253-20244-2   pa.
2 3 4 5 83 82 81 80

For Mom and Dad

James Homer and Mae Moore Flynt

CONTENTS

ILLUSTRATIONS

Foreword

The idea for this series of books took shape a decade ago, when the editors were colleagues at the University of Georgia. Our memorable luncheon gatherings, which frequently included Willard Gatewood, Melvin Herndon, Charles Alexander, Bob Griffith, Roger Nichols, Emory Thomas, and Will Holmes, were filled with anecdotal testimonials about our own histories. The two of us were fascinated by one another's provincialism—one having become a young adult before meeting a northerner or a Jew or a Catholic, the other having moved to Georgia without ever riding a mule or attending a revival. It has increasingly occurred to us that what one teaches about American history and what students learn in American history courses are strongly related (probably rightly so) to the location of one's university. Students in Alabama who have never seen a subway, or much of an urban ghetto, or a first-generation immigrant still flock to courses on the Civil War. And New Jersey classes are filled with students who have never seen a cotton field, a Klansman, or a mimosa tree. So one person's American history centers on the Taft-Hartley Act, while another's defines the Wheeler-Howard Act, the Tennessee Valley Authority, or the gay rights movement as the central issue of the American experience. We need to understand ourselves, but if we would know our country, we must do more.

This series of books studies one key level of American loyalties, the numerous and often ill-defined minority groups that exist in fact or in myth. In the broadest sense humans identify with the common sufferings and aspirations of all mankind. On a second level we relate our self-interest to our nation. When confronted with a foreign environment (as the editors experienced during their Fulbright years in India and Spain), even those of us who would not think of ourselves as superpatriots become self-consciously aware of how American we are. At the other end of the spectrum, all of us identify our self-interest in personal and family terms. In short, all of us have complex loyalties, but most Americans identify with some group (or groups) larger than family and smaller than nation, groups defined by section, class, race, sex, or ideology. It is that identification which shapes our most immediate value judgments.

Nearly thirty years ago Walter Prescott Webb argued that the closing of world frontiers spelled the end of the individualistic days of Western civilization. The fluidity of a society in economic boom would be replaced by the stasis of a society that emphasized order and stability. Men in the West would increasingly come to identify with groups, slowly abandoning the emphasis on individualism and all its free-wheeling implications. Webb's view, of course, contradicts the more commonly held belief that most people have always seen themselves as part of some important larger group. Whichever assertion is correct, the history of America is a unique case study in the survival and molding of group loyalties. Remarkable and important as the rise of nationalism in the United States has been, all Americans—even the most affluent and powerful—have, in some sense, remained hyphenated. The founding fathers' vision of a competing and compromising balance of minorities has come much closer to being realized than has the later ideal of a melting pot.

The most common focus of group unity has been ethnic. Race or place of origin was particularly central to the lives of the late arrivals in America, who found that ethnic groups generally shared homogeneous economic, social, and cultural values. But Americans have consciously sought to go beyond the confines of ethnic-group loyalty. The ethnic dimension has become less central, particularly in the mainstream of American life, where millions of people care little about their genealogies. But other important associations have been formed. Regional loyalties seem ineradicable. Many people also identify themselves with an economic class. At times that identification has been quite broad—the poor or the middle class—but more often people hold a stronger identification with a specific economic group, such as industrial workers or the urban poor. Finally, some people's view of the world is shaped primarily by intellectual and cultural values. One might be poor and black and southern and yet live as a Christian zealot, a Marxist, or a cynic. In short, all of us are many things, but at any given time we are likely to hold some loyalty supreme, or at least vitally important. It is those loyalties, those minority-group identifications, which this series seeks to examine, explain, and evaluate.

In this volume Professor Wayne Flynt, head of the History Department at Auburn University, introduces us to a nebulous but hardy group of Americans—poor southern whites. Both Wayne Flynt and Ed Harrell know them well. Southern poor whites have seldom been a united or politically active group, yet they have shared a culture and sense of values. Millions of modern middle-class southerners consciously and proudly trace their roots to "redneck" ancestors and, consciously or unconsciously, owe much of their character to that heritage. As Professor Flynt shows, poor southern whites are still a prominent and puzzling social problem for the nation. Off and on, outsiders have become aware of southern poor whites as a distinctive class, sometimes viewing them with disdain and derision and sometimes with sympathy and reforming zeal. This book tells us something of Dixie's forgotten poor, of how they have seen themselves and how others have understood them, of what has been done for them and to them by the larger society. So read on, to learn of dogtrots and lining hymns and clay-eating and other American customs and tribulations that flourished on the red-clay farms, the wooded hills, and in the mill towns of the South.

David Edwin Harrell, Jr.
Birmingham, Alabama

Warren F. Kimball
Somerset, New Jersey

Preface

We had finished our oral history project and Mrs. L. A. House sat with shoulders sagging from eighty-nine years of labor as tenant farmer and textile worker. The memories had been painful: married at fourteen, widowed in her twenties, she had buried three husbands, three of her five children, eight brothers and sisters. With eyes focused on the floor she said, more to herself than to me, "It's been a hard life." Then, with a twinkle that belongs to her alone, she lifted her head and looked firmly at me: "But it hasn't been all bad either."

The bittersweet life of white poor people in the South is the topic of this book. Viewing them as an ethnic minority may seem strange because they appear to be the quintessence of America: Protestant residents of the Bible Belt, mostly Anglo-Saxon in origin, part of the most ethnically homogeneous region of America. Yet, the definition of "ethnic group" applied by Salvatore J. LaGumina and Frank J. Cavaioli in 1974 fits the Southern poor white almost as well as it does the "new immigrants" whom they discussed. LaGumina and Cavaioli wrote that ethnicity consisted of a group of racially and historically related people who shared a common culture which they preserved in a distinctive way of life, language, habit, and loyalty. Evaluated by such a standard, Southern poor whites obviously are a distinct group. This definition also clarified the designation "poor white." Some poor who live in the South—blacks, eastern and southern European immigrants, and Chicanos—do not share the common and distinctive culture of Anglo whites and are not a part of this discussion.

Definitions of ethnicity took on a new importance during the decade of the 1960s when America confronted its own internal diversity as never before. Talk of a "pluralistic society" constructed from the pieces of "ethnic subcultures" constituted one way of making sense out of that tumultuous era. Sociologist Lewis M. Killian authored a book on *White Southerners* as part of a series entitled "Ethnic Groups in Comparative Perspective." Although he did not distinguish "white southerners" by economic category, his most convincing chapter, "White Southern Migrants," concerned the problems of poor white "hillbillies" in Northern cities. There they fell prey to the same kinds of stereotypes, visibility problems (their accent gave them away as certainly as the names of eastern and southern European immigrants), and discrimination that have plagued other ethnics. Although Killian argued that they experienced greater social mobility than blacks, they were burdened by the same kinds of problems.

John Shelton Reed's *The Enduring South: Subculture Persistence in Mass Society* (1972) utilized opinion polls to argue the same point. He concluded that Southerners were more likely to be conventionally religious, to accept the use of force, and to draw meaning from their family roots. These attitudes have become stronger in recent years.

Finally, Professor George B. Tindall examined these same issues in his witty, forceful presidential address to the 1973 Southern Historical Association. His Atlanta speech, "Beyond the Mainstream: The Ethnic Southerners," spoke of a unique brand of rebel who remained outside the American consensus. Published under the title *The Ethnic Southerners* (1976), this enlarged essay elaborated many of the insights offered by Reed.

None of these approaches to ethnicity focused exclusively on poor whites. Obviously, such people do share much in common with their regional companions of the middle and upper classes. Yet, as C. Vann Woodward reminded us so forcefully in *The Burden of Southern History,* the ethnic experience of most Southerners was a quite un-American relationship with poverty; and the poor remain more easily ignored and negatively stereotyped than the relatively affluent. If all white Southerners have shared to some extent in a common ethnic experience, that experience has been all the more significant for the poor among them. Their isolation from mainstream culture has been more complete, their economic and political powerlessness more debilitating. Poor whites have been in turn stereotyped by the dominant culture (as rednecks, Holy Rollers), discriminated against, and misunderstood. In their isolation, poor whites have developed a unique subculture; they have defended it with a tenacity and pride that puzzles and confuses the larger society. When the federal government offered poverty programs and sought to integrate poor Southerners into the mainstream, the objects of such help often responded like nonwestern developing nations, telling the United States to take its aid and go to hell. The economic integration of Southern poor whites must respect the unique culture which they formed over time.

Getting to know people as individuals dissolves many of one's preconceived notions about them, and so it is with Southern poor whites. For one who has lived with them and come to understand them, stereotypes give way to individual differences. Differences, in turn, take on values, and one has to weigh carefully credits and debits. Not every characteristic of poor whites speaks of nobility, endurance, courage, and faith. Present also is violence, racism, oversimplification of complicated economic and social issues, resistance to change, and apathy. But greater understanding clarifies and qualifies even these ignoble traits.

My thanks go to many persons who assisted this study, especially to my wife Dorothy and to the staffs of the Samford University library and the Auburn University Archives. To former colleagues in the Samford University history department, especially David Vess, Jim Brown, and Leah Atkins, I owe much. My student secretary at Samford University, Dan Cloyd, served the role of editorial assistant as much as he did typist. Sherri Sherwood, head secretary of the history department at Auburn University, performed in her usual proficient manner typing the final manuscript. Warren F. Kimball of Rutgers University and David Edwin Harrell, Jr., of the University of Alabama in Birmingham, editors of the series of which this volume is a part, provided rigorous but invaluable critiques. Most of all my thanks go to Mr. and Mrs. L. A. House, from whom I learned so much about the powerful religion of poor white carpenters and textile workers, and to my father and mother, James and Mae Moore Flynt, who reintroduced me to my own roots among the proud sharecroppers of the northeast Alabama clay hills.

CHAPTER ONE

THE INVISIBLE POOR
Toward a Definition of Southern Poor Whites

In one of the essays that periodically appear on the "problem South," historian Paul Buck admonished: "If ever there was a region which should write its history in terms of the strivings of its common folk, it seems to me it is the South." Viewing society from the vantage point of the mudsill, however, seldom has been the historical approach. Social scientists, in fact, have been unable to agree on a definition of the common people, much less to write from their perspective.

One difficulty in defining poor whites stems from the diverse ways in which the phrase has been used. It has been applied to economic and social classes as well as to cultural and ethical values. Poor whites have been characterized as degenerate racists, white trash commonly guilty of incest and mindless violence. Primitive and illiterate, they supposedly bequeathed no legacy to music, literature, art, or architecture. Their society was clannish and closed to outsiders, who were objects of suspicion and fear. Economically, they were impoverished people who lived a marginal existence. Unfortunately, when attempts have been made to quantify these vague assumptions, more confusion than clarity has resulted. Most Southern poor whites were racists, but the expressions of their prejudices were contradictory and require explanation. Some poor whites hated blacks so much that they allied with conservative white planters whose economic interests were antithetical to their own, while others participated in the Populist biracial coalition of the 1890s. An antebellum Southern poor white was defined by one group of historians as someone who did not own land; later scholars insisted that many landless common folk possessed substantial wealth in the form of livestock. In recent years, poverty has been used to refer both to a specific economic condition (an income of less than three thousand dollars for a family of four) and to a more general state in which a person is denied access to power. Economics, the most quantifiable definition, has not produced statistical data that can be consistently applied to reveal how many poor whites there were in 1861 or even 1932. To explore all these elements would constitute tome and not essay, and would leave the reader more confused than enlightened.

The narrower focus of the following pages will explore chiefly two aspects of Southern poor white experience: their economic condition and their culture. The first task is the simpler of the two, for without exception these people were economically powerless. The statistical definition of poverty changed with time, but they always lived on the margin, with a bare minimum of land, calories, education, medical care, worldly goods, and security. Their material problems were inextricably linked to politics; the more affluent Southerners who directed the South's political destiny were often apathetic or hostile to their poorer neighbors, which infrequently provoked poor whites to seek elusive salvation in political protest. Such efforts brought little relief.

Southern poor white culture is a happier saga to relate. Despite overwhelmingly negative stereotypes, which usually depicted them as culturally sterile and degenerate, the most compelling aspect of their culture was its differentness. This difference, sometimes diminishing and othertimes enriching the quality of Southern life, demands serious exploration by anyone who seeks to understand these people. During decades of wretchedness and abysmal deprivation, a distinctive culture emerged to help them make sense out of their condition and maintain some dignity. When labor unionism and an expanding Southern economy permitted passage into the promised land of lower middle-class prosperity, they carried their culture with them, somewhat adapted to fit the new, more sophisticated reality, but nonetheless recognizable whether in the form of country music or emotional religion.

Because shifting American attitudes toward Southern poor whites play a central role in both their early isolation and their more recent mobility, such opinions cannot be ignored. Forays into popular literature are not detours from the main story, but are essential to the narrative. Since their fate was so often in the hands of the "better classes," it is imperative that one understand how mainstream Americans perceived poor whites, how such stereotypes changed over time, and ultimately how a literature sympathetic toward them allowed the evolution of programs designed to improve their lives. Because they were so often economically and politically powerless, their salvation had to come from above. Although their culture provided the spiritual resources necessary to keep them from despair and degradation, material assistance waited for an era of social consciousness when the realization of their suffering pricked the American conscience and moved it to action. Unfortunately, the mainstream's solution was conceived in its own culture and value system and lifted the poor more often into purgatory than into the heavenly city.

If historian C. Vann Woodward is correct in his assumption that the South's distinctiveness is grounded partly in its long experience with poverty within a nation celebrated for affluence, then obviously the poor have played a key role in defining the South. In his seminal work, *The Burden of Southern History,* Woodward reminded that poverty was no "temporary misfortune" for the South, but a "continuous and conspicuous feature of Southern experience." With such an admonition, only the complexity of the problems has kept Southerners so ignorant of their own roots, which derive more frequently from antebellum poor than from plantation grandees.

Defining the South is a simpler task, although the meaning of the term also changed over time. Applied to the antebellum period, the South generally refers to the eleven states from Virginia to Texas that constituted the Confederacy in 1861. Following the war, the definition becomes more economic and cultural than political; hence, the addition of Kentucky, West Virginia, and Oklahoma to the region.[1]

The years before the Civil War, those romanticized decades symbolized by magnificent Georgian architecture and a glamorous aristocracy, were not so happy for tens of thousands of white Southerners. How many poor existed has become obscured in a seemingly endless debate. The earliest accounts of Northern travelers through the region created the inaccurate impression that the white South was a two-class society made up of planters and poor whites. The abolitionist ideology of some travelers, such as historian Frederick Law Olmsted who journeyed through the region in the 1850s, led them to conclude that the lower class was impoverished, not by sterile soil, but by the evil institution of slavery. Poor whites avoided work because they identified physical labor with black slaves.

This simplistic image of antebellum Southern society eventually was altered by a more complex description. Many white Southerners had appeared to be poor because they owned no land, but this conclusion was erroneous. Actually, many of them were herdsmen, owners of large numbers of hogs and cattle, which foraged in the forests until ready for transportation to Eastern or Midwestern markets. Numerically there were more white Southerners found in this category of yeoman than in either the planter or poor white classes. The yeoman owned no slaves, grew enough crops to be self-sufficient in food production, and experienced so much economic mobility that he oftentimes became a planter. Although the yeoman class developed its own folk culture of crafts, tools, architecture, festivals, and religious institutions, it possessed no well-defined sense of class consciousness. Yeomen admired planters, shared their racial views, and expected to become aristocrats themselves someday. Many yeomen obtained rudimentary education in some 2,500 academies scattered across the South; they demanded a role in Southern politics; and they were individualistic in their religion and crafts.

This more complex and accurate description of a three-tiered so-

ciety still left unresolved the extent of material poverty. Although some
yeomen entered the planter class in the decade of the 1850s, many
small farmers were forced on to wornout land. As antebellum Southern
towns developed, other whites moved off the land and took menial, low-
paying industrial jobs. In Hancock County, Georgia, one-third of the
total white population belonged to the bottom class during the 1850s.
Some of them were tenant farmers who owned no real estate or property and subsisted on hunting and fishing. Others were textile mill operatives whose wages were so low that many women and children had
to work. These factory workers stood lowest on the economic ladder.
As early as 1787 the majority of adult males in the state of Virginia
owned no land. By 1860, there were between 300,000 and 400,000
white persons living in poverty in the four states of Virginia, North and
South Carolina, and Georgia. Within these South Atlantic states, poor
whites constituted as much as one-fifth of the total white population.

Society assumed little if any responsibility for such folk. Some
Southern counties provided relief in kind or doles. Operation of the
poor laws must have been similar to a case in Bradley County, Arkansas: "Come Abadiah Walker and shows the Court that he is a citizen
of this county and that he is to all intentions and purposes a pauper and
prays the Court for an appropriation. Thereupon the Court grants said
prayer and orders that the sum of $12 be appropriated to said pauper
for the term."[2]

That not all indigents were so fortunate as Abadiah Walker is plain
from an 1800 account by Michael Gaffney. Taking leave of his fashionable Charleston, South Carolina, residence, Gaffney traveled across
the upland region to Spartanburg, recording the inhospitable life of the
poor.

> The country for about one hundred and fifty miles from Charleston
> is extremely low and unhealthy. The people looked yellow, poor, and
> sickly. Some of them lived the most miserably I ever saw any poor
> people live. We arrived at our new home in six days. I expected to see
> a fine country but was surprised to find it poor, sandy, rocky and hilly.
> The people are poor. Their dress generally is a hunting shirt and trou-

sers of coarse cotton yarn. . . . The women of this country live the poorest lives of any people in the world. It is directly opposite to Charleston; here they must do everything from cooking to plowing and after that they have no more life in them than Indian squaws.[3]

Obviously, the range of deprivation and the sense of hopelessness that sometimes accompanied it differed even within states. A poor antebellum family living on virgin soil in a frontier region or in the mountains with ample wild life enjoyed a better life than a family living in an older agricultural community; but both were poor.

As important as the determination of how many whites were indigent is the more interpretive question of why they were poor. Obviously, the explanation is not to be found in their ethnic origin for it was similar to that of their more affluent neighbors. Like planters, poor whites were mostly of British and Scottish stock, and few could be traced to the limited convict immigration of colonial times. The poor whites of the 1850s had descended from the yeomen or even from slaveholders of an earlier period. Downward mobility was more characteristic of their experience than upward movement.

The causes of this decline were related to land distribution and utilization as well as to sloth and ignorance. In newly opened areas of the antebellum South, such as Alabama, Mississippi, Louisiana, and Arkansas, rapid settlement encouraged wasteful overcultivation. With so much land available on the Southern frontier, planters and farmers concentrated on maximizing profits. They invested little of their capital in maintaining soil productivity because it was cheaper to buy and improve new land than to take care of old. Planters moving south and west to new plots left behind a trail of farmed-out soil that became the home of poor whites. Virgin land in hill regions quickly eroded and also reduced sturdy yeomen to impoverished subsistence farmers.

Technology, an ever-present villain in the story of the Southern common folk, played a role in the origins of the poor white class. Invention of the cotton gin in 1793 changed the patterns of land distribution. Small farms were consolidated into more productive and efficient plantations. Yeomen often resisted this consolidation, but economic conditions frequently forced them to sell. Newspapers in South Carolina and Georgia were filled with advertisements of sheriff's sales of land during the frequent depressions. Development of the cotton gin and the plantation system, which arose because of it, also created an economic order that resisted technological change. The plantation economy did not require the technology of transportation, communication, industry, and finance that developed in other regions and that elsewhere provided economic mobility for poor whites.

Historians, Northern abolitionists, and even some antebellum Southerners such as Hinton Helper blamed slavery for the presence of so many dispossessed whites. In the slave economy, Negroes monopolized agricultural and nonagricultural jobs. Planters rented out their skilled slaves who competed with whites. Blacks, both slave and free, were also prominent in coal mining and the textile industry. The presence of slave labor, together with the poor white sense of racial superiority, also placed a stigma on certain types of labor; some students of poor whites argued that slavery stigmatized *all* forms of physical labor in the South and produced a lower class of whites who were lazy and shiftless.

More exotic explanations for Southern white poverty have provided enduring stereotypes. Some within the planter class charged that lower-class whites were biologically inferior; antebellum poor whites were often depicted as depraved, odd, and garish. In the classic phrase of one nameless critic, "poor whites were born lazy and had a relapse." Some early twentieth century health specialists laid the blame to the debilitating maladies of the poor: malaria, hookworm, clay-eating. As late as 1947, Edgar T. Thompson, a Duke University professor, wrote in a leading sociology journal that hookworm was only symptomatic of the social and economic traditions of poor whites. Their purposelessness resulted from "improvidence, moral degeneracy, lack of ambition, and indifference to profitable labor." He compared poor whites unfavorably to the remarkable progress being made by blacks: "the general conclusion is, in my opinion, inescapable; the poor whites somewhere along the line suffered a failure of nerve and lost purpose; Negroes, on the contrary, came without purpose but are gaining it."

While there were degenerates among poor whites, the only universal characteristic was their common poverty. Many poor whites were paupers; others held menial jobs. Illiteracy was common. The superintendent of the federal census of 1850 announced a native white illiteracy rate of 20.3 percent in the slave states, 3 percent in the Middle states, and .42 percent in New England. The diet of many whites may have been more deficient than that of slaves. One estimate of the most common ration of corn for a slave family of five was sixty-five bushels per year. Based on the recorded production of the 128 poorest white farmers in Edgefield County, South Carolina, their actual corn production fell well below this minimum.

Many poor whites already had begun to move to town. For generations historians assumed that they moved toward the mountains, and there was westward mobility, especially within the South Atlantic region. But they also moved to towns, many of which showed an increase in laborers and unemployed family heads during the 1850s. In antebellum New Orleans, for instance, three out of every five residents were poor. Antebellum factory workers, concentrated mainly in towns and cities, were at or near the bottom of the socioeconomic ladder. Textile workers sometimes worked twelve hours a day for a daily wage of only ten cents. At Graniteville, South Carolina, where William Gregg hoped that his textile mills would revitalize the poor white community, there were 287 operatives in 1860. Just 51 were adult heads of families; the rest were boys and girls, mostly girls.

Of course many poor whites also could be found in mountainous regions, but there was a tendency among yeomen and planters to exempt them from the category of Southern poor whites. Such exclusion emphasized the multidimensional meanings of poverty. When antebellum planters, yeomen, or blacks used the phrase "poor white," the term connoted moral and material degeneracy, as in "po' white trash." Mountain people might be economically impoverished, but they retained a consciousness of ancestry, a pride in their unique culture, their oral traditions, legends, and stories. They were recognized as part of a folk society that produced aesthetically pleasing and useful crafts and maintained viable folk institutions. By contrast, no such redeeming contributions were attributed to lowland poor whites, who were considered to be rootless, shiftless people alienated even from their own ethnic kind. Such games played with semantics allowed antebellum society to negatively stereotype some impoverished whites, while exempting others.

As used in antebellum society, "Southern poor white" became a sociocultural term describing a broader frame of character, rather than an economic term depicting a lack of material well-being. One statement of folk wisdom tried in vain to clarify: "All whites who are poor are not *poor whites.*" Over the years other euphemisms developed to join the onerous term "poor white": *rednecks, hillbillies, sand hillers, wooly hats, crackers.* Often these terms were related to geography or to articles of clothing (farmers often wore wide-brimmed wool hats when laboring in the blistering sun). Sometimes the origin of a term was more obscure as with cracker, which came into wide usage in south Georgia and north Florida, then spread elsewhere. The word "cracker" has been attributed to the antebellum practice of poor whites living in the pine forests of pounding their own corn before mills were constructed. Others believed that the term originated among town dwellers who called country folk crackers because they cracked their long whips when driving their oxen or mules into town. One sociologist traced the term to the seventeenth-century derivation of cracker, which denoted "bomb" and referred to the explosive temperament of the nineteenth-century frontier class.

Whatever the origin of the word, cracker culture owed much to the economic conditions of a frozen frontier characterized by static technology and geographical isolation. These economic implications are equally implicit in redneck, hillbilly, and the other terms applied to Southern poor whites.

Beginning in the 1930s, the economic explanation for antebellum white poverty began to dominate scholarly debate. Sociologists especially divided the South's pre-Civil War whites into those who participated in the economic system and those who were so poor that they raised nothing for the market. Planters, yeoman farmers, and Negro slaves functioned within the economic system. Poor whites had nothing to sell except their labor, and the market for that was largely closed to them by the presence of slaves. Stranded on worn-out sand hills, in pine barrens, or in remote mountains, they lived on the edge of subsistence by hunting, fishing, or by raising meager crops and a few hogs. Sometimes members of this class functioned within the economic system by doing odd jobs for wages, as tenants on land owned by planters, or as mill workers; but these were not customary roles for poor whites. Bare economic subsistence and isolation were more typical. This exclusion from the mainstream carried a definite caste image. The status of poor whites was fixed and inferior. Since they lacked a chance to participate in the division of labor, they had no way of securing a share of the goods and services that the economy produced. This economic argument was modified somewhat in the 1940s by historians who emphasized the abundant livestock possessed by many landless whites.

Physical isolation also caused the white poor to be shut out of the institutional life of the community, thus molding them into a cultural pattern easily stereotyped as different from that of the whites who participated fully in the economy. Certain cultural traits were thought common to them (lazy, shiftless, ignorant). The next step, of course, was to explain the existence of the lower class as the outgrowth of these cultural factors (they were poor because they were lazy, shiftless, ignorant).

If the isolation and poverty of poor whites resulted from the operation of the plantation economy, one would expect to discover class conflict in the antebellum South. Yet most students of the antebellum South agree that while class division existed, there was little class conflict, particularly between poor whites and the dominant classes. Poor whites shared the racial views of the aristocracy, and believed the plantation system to be superior to the commercial economy of the North. There are many explanations for this common purpose. There was enough mobility that poor whites hoped to become yeomen and perhaps even planters. Americans characteristically are not class conscious. Also, many poor whites were distantly related to yeomen and planters, or at least assumed such kinship. Even the poor white dislike of manual toil reflected an aristocratic attitude of that day. To Northern attacks on the South's laziness, the Southern aristocracy responded that the slower pace of life came from a more leisurely society that contrasted favorably to the money-grubbing materialism of Yankee commercial life. Exploitation is a major source of class conflict, and poor whites generally were neither exploited nor mistreated by the aristocracy; they were simply ignored.

Since poor whites were not overtly oppressed, they shared the dominant view toward blacks, which in turn caused them to defend Southern institutions. In some respects, poor whites were harsher racists than yeomen or planters. Since slaves were an important part of the economic system and enjoyed greater material security, poor whites could take pride only in color. Poor whites showed no hesitation in accepting all three assumptions on which white supremacy was based: (1) it was part of the natural order; (2) the Negro was inferior to the white; (3) any decline in white superiority would lead to racial amalgamation. Virtually all Southern whites shared these views, but poor whites defended them most emotionally and violently.

On this point a major debate has raged for years. Some scholars insisted that in the South white class interests were subordinated to race interests. A Marxist class interpretation, they argued, cannot explain the hold that slavery had on the Southern white because nonslaveholders perceived no conflict between their interests and those of planters. Also, planters were divided in their own economic and political philosophies.

The major historical spokesman for a distinctive class-oriented way of life, Eugene Genovese, argued that the antebellum South was a unique, prebourgeois society fundamentally different from the North. A self-conscious and unified planter class ruled this society by infusing its own values throughout the social order. Secession was a reasoned, logical result of the planter's thought and the only way of maintaining his class status. The condition of yeomen and poor whites was not improving in the 1850s, and historical estimates concerning the size and prosperity of the yeoman class made in the 1940s were exaggerated. Other historians have challenged this conception of a monolithic and self-conscious planter class, and have questioned the extent of economic class division in the antebellum South.

Pre-Civil War Southern politics provided one test of the extent of class division, although it is impossible to separate poor white from middle-class yeomen, so similar were their common interests. Despite white unity on questions of race, the economic isolation of poor whites and limited opportunities for yeomen eventually caused class antagonisms. This discontent led to a political revolt in which poor whites joined yeomen in an attempt to wrest leadership away from the gentry. Hinton Rowan Helper became the most extreme spokesman for this group in the late 1850s. Although a white racist himself, he condemned the effect of slavery on poor whites. Helper's appeal won no response from poor whites who were oftentimes illiterate; his ideas had little circulation in the South, and he was forced to move North. Despite his personal failure to influence the bottom class, poverty had caused poor whites to grow restive. Aristocratic resistance to public education, welfare, and land reform caused many yeomen and poor whites to vote for candidates who appealed to their classes and interests.

Political debate provided a platform for the discussion of class issues. Before the Civil War, Southern whites voted as frequently as Northerners. This was due partly to the appearance of a number of white demagogues who appealed along class lines to poorer white voters. People who were isolated, ignored, powerless, and emotionally starved often followed a charismatic figure, whether preacher of politician. The demagogues appealed mostly to poor whites who lived in the pine barrens of south central Georgia or east of the Pearl River in Mississippi, and to the people clustered in the sand hills and abandoned clay bottoms of South Carolina, Alabama, and Florida. Poor whites exercised their greatest influence in the new states of the Southwest (Alabama, Mississippi, Louisiana) rather than in the older, more politically stable South Atlantic states such as Virginia and the Carolinas.

The political demagogue burst into the drab existence of the poor white like an emotional, August camp meeting revivalist. Franklin E. Plummer emerged in the early 1830s as the spokesman for the piney woods poor of east Mississippi against the planters of the Delta counties. His attempts to unite poor workingmen, farmers, and herdsmen against the rich attracted favorable notice in northeastern working-men's newspapers and raised class feelings to unprecedented levels in Mississippi. In Jacksonian fashion, he opposed recharter of the Bank of the United States and endorsed internal improvements, state taxation favoring small farmers, and construction of a state school in every county. Elected to Congress by his poor white constituency, he soon deserted them for the Natchez banking interests. His apostasy cost him his piney woods constituency, and he lost his bid for a United States Senate seat.

Plummer had many imitators. Albert Gallatin Brown greatly admired Plummer and in many ways duplicated his career. Born in South Carolina to poverty-stricken parents, he grew up in the Mississippi piney woods. He championed the interests of small nonslaveholding farmers against Delta planters and Natchez bankers. He combined racist rhetoric with advocacy of east Mississippi poor white interests to win the common folk who elected him governor, congressman, and senator in the 1850s. Across the Tombigbee River in Alabama, W. R. W. Cobb won a seat in Congress by appealing to a similar constituency. Anticipating such country music groups as the Strawberry Pickers who would entertain audiences more than a century later for Governors James E. Folsom and George C. Wallace, Cobb relied on singing to appeal to his earthy constituency. He began his rallies with a favorite ditty entitled "Uncle Sam is Rich Enough to Give Us All a Farm." He would wink as he sang, pausing occasionally to chew a piece of onion and some coarse pone bread.

Such frank support of poor white causes did result in improvements. Most Southern states established systems of poor relief and schools for the poor during the 1820s and 1830s. On the eve of the Civil War the Southern states also had prohibited imprisonment for debts, regulated banks, and provided uniform and equal taxation of property. The years from 1776 to 1860 saw the masses of whites, especially yeomen, gaining political influence.

One example of the issue orientation of poor whites and yeomen can be seen in their support for homestead legislation. Although many Southern congressmen from the planter class opposed enactment of a homestead bill in the years prior to 1861, some of their Southern colleagues favored free land. Most of these pro-homestead congressmen were of plain folk origin and represented mountainous, pine-barren, or piney woods districts. The first man to suggest the homestead concept in Congress was Franklin Plummer of Mississippi, and Alabamian W. R. W. Cobb and others like him were strong advocates of free land.

The fate of homestead legislation characterized the tragic political betrayal of poor whites. Although they won a voice in the political system, the demagogues they elected often deserted them. Blocked both by aristocratic Southern opposition and by the defection of some demagogic leaders, the homestead act failed to pass Congress until after the South seceded.

Other reform movements that might have improved the condition of poor whites also met political defeat. Only North Carolina and Kentucky created a system of schools sufficiently complete to resemble public education. In other states common schools generally were charity institutions, and the stigma repelled many proud whites who allowed their children to grow up illiterate rather than acknowledge their poverty. The South lagged far behind other sections in the provision for public welfare, and the political leadership of the region generally assumed that if one could not provide for himself, he deserved his fate. Common whites, so long ignored, gained a modicum of political power, only to see self-serving demagogues of their own class betray them. The Jacksonian revolution that had dawned so brightly gave way to the 1840s and '50s and steadily increasing poverty in the clay bottoms, swamps, and pine barrens.

CHAPTER TWO

DOGTROTS AND JACK TALES
Toward a Definition of
Poor White Culture

Arnold Toynbee, British historian of world civilizations, managed to find space in his massive work, *A Study of History,* for the Scotch-Irish of the Southern mountains. Comparing poor Appalachian whites to their ethnic counterparts in Ulster, Northern Ireland, two centuries after they had parted company, Toynbee wrote:

> The modern Appalachian has not only not improved on the Ulster-man; he has failed to hold his ground and has gone downhill in a most disconcerting fashion. In fact, the Appalachian 'mountain people' today are no better than barbarians. They have relapsed into illiteracy and witchcraft. They suffer from poverty, squalor and ill-health. They are the American counterparts of the latter-day white barbarians of the Old World—Rifis, Albanians, Kurds, Pathans, and Hairy Ainus; but, whereas these latter are belated survivals of an ancient barbarism, the Appalachians present the melancholy spectacle of a people who have acquired civilization and then lost it.[1]

If so eminent an authority as Toynbee could be so badly confused about Southern poor white culture, it is no wonder that less erudite

Americans made the same mistake. The critical error of judgment was concluding that material indigence found its equivalent in poverty of the spirit.

In areas remote from stimulating cities such as Charleston, South Carolina, generations of the antebellum poor produced a culture that met their basic needs, that was aesthetically pleasing, and that may still be enjoyed by Southerners seeking their own roots. It was common to most of the subregions of the South. Although Appalachia diverged from the South in significant ways after the Civil War, poor white antebellum culture was essentially similar. Much of this culture was shared by Southerners of the yeoman class. Yeoman and poor white worshipped in the same Primitive Baptist churches, attended the same camp meetings, strummed the same tunes on dulcimer and banjo, recited the same ghost stories and tall tales, and constructed the same kinds of cabins. Other aspects of poor white culture were unique to them. No doubt a degenerate residue of whites functioned outside this culture; but to ignore poor white folk culture is to rob them of an integral part of their history.

A world fast using up its resources should appreciate a folk culture that maintained a remarkable harmony with its environment. Southern poor whites lived by an ethic of repair or mend; their isolation and poverty forced them to make what they needed. Folk crafts and architecture were ingenious in their economy and simplicity, yet they frequently incorporated a satisfying aesthetic quality.

Function was the dominant feature in all folk crafts, whether the use of scraps of cloth to make a quilt, or the design of houses. The characteristic architecture of the nineteenth-century South was not the fabled mansion but the lowly log cabin and dogtrot house. The dogtrot consisted of two rooms at either end of an open breezeway, while the log cabin was a simple one room structure made of logs, which were hewed by ax, fitted at the ends, and cracks between them chinked with a mixture of straw and clay. These simple structures demonstrated the ingenuity of common people who built homes with little money, limited materials, and no formal training as builders. Skills were passed from generation to generation with little variation in basic design or tools, although subregional variety appeared in both structure and building materials. The folk building bore an organic relation to its environment, using materials that were indigenous to the area. A dog-trot house in the piney woods was constructed of pine split into huge boards; the same structure in the Mississippi Delta was built from cypress logs. Both were chinked with mud, and topped by shingles split by the use of a tool called a froe. The dogtrot construction allowed maximum ventilation during the oppressively hot summer months and could be added onto with ease. The dogtrot and the transverse crib barn, which it inspired, appeared throughout the southern Appalachians, the Cumberland Mountains, and the North Carolina Piedmont in the years before the Civil War.

Although function counted most in folk crafts, the aesthetic was not ignored. The quilt was symbolic of a process by which the craftsman could unite useless objects into beautiful new forms. Pieces of cloth, which a more affluent society discarded, were sewn into a kaleidoscope of color and pattern. Just as quilts combined practical needs with elaborate and creative folk designs, the houses of the poor served a dual purpose. Both the exterior and interior of houses exhibited a sense of texture, space, and design. Many of the building materials were salvage items. Worn out horseshoes were bent and pins inserted to make hinges. Newspapers were used to paper the inside of the house. Furnishings were made from grape and honeysuckle vines, from reed and white oak trees. One nameless craftsman spoke eloquently for generations of the South's poor when he described his creation: "It's a shape of something that never has been presented. No one has ever seen that. It was in my mind and spirit to do that. It represents some of the things in the earth that people been throwing away for years."[2]

If folk crafts represented one of the most affirmative statements of poor white culture, antebellum literature contains one of the most demeaning. American writers seem always to be creating their own images of poor whites, a fact inextricably connected to the fate of the class. From Virginia aristocrat William Byrd to Northern abolitionist Harriet Beecher Stowe, authors used poor whites to serve their own ideological purposes. One of the South's first novelists, William Gilmore Simms, depicted them as villains. Stowe's *Uncle Tom's Cabin* exaggerated the extent of the poorer class and reduced poor whites to listless squatters or barbarous "nigger catchers."

The Southwestern humorists, writing about the newly opened antebellum frontier in Mississippi and Alabama, corrected such caricatures by more realistically depicting the class. The laughter that the humorists attributed to poor whites humanized the harsh and tragic characters who appeared in Stowe and Simms. They mercifully omitted social commentary, for their task was to record types of humor and to amuse. Their stories portrayed a difficult but meaningful life that was a lively, democratic contrast to the elegant romance of the planter class. They recorded lives that were sometimes harmless, othertimes belligerent, often joyous and exciting.

The prose of the Southwestern humorists provided a social portrait of a raw, individualistic poor white subculture. These stories sparkled with descriptions of the wit and vibrant life of the poor. Although not themselves a part of the bottom class, the best of the humorists—David Crockett in his *Autobiography,* Augustus Baldwin Longstreet's *Georgia Scenes,* Johnson J. Hooper's *Simon Suggs' Adventures* —provided remarkable insights into poor white culture. "The Fight," a folk classic by Longstreet describing brutal combat between Billy Stallions and Bob Durham, was not only an accurate portrayal of violent poor white society, but also a marvelously descriptive example of the kind of tales that poor whites told among themselves. Ransy Sniffle, protagonist of the story, maneuvered Stallions and Durham into an eye-gouging wrestling match:

> Now there happened to reside in the county . . . a little fellow by the name of Ransy Sniffle: a sprout of Richmond, who in his early days, had fed copiously upon red clay and blackberries. This diet had given to Ransy a complexion that a corpse would have disdained to own, and an abdominal rotundity that was quite unprepossessing. Long spells of the fever and ague, too, in Ransy's youth had conspired with clay and blackberries to throw him quite out of the order of nature. His shoulders were fleshless and elevated; his head large and flat; his neck slim and translucent; and his arms, hands, fingers, and feet were lengthened out of all proportion to the rest of his frame. His joints

were large and his limbs small; and as for flesh, he could not, with propriety, be said to have any. Those parts which nature usually supplies with the most of this article—the calves of the legs, for example—presented in him the appearance of so many well-drawn blisters. His height was just five feet nothing; and his average weight in blackberry season, ninety-five.[3]

Here too were insights into the social customs of poor whites and how their mores diverged from the larger society. Longstreet's description of Sniffle provided information on diet, health, and qualities of shrewdness and trickery that were esteemed among the poor. Antebellum Alabama humorist Johnson Hooper created a mischievous boy whom he called Yellow-legs. The lad heckled Simon Suggs until Suggs finally confronted him: "I'll kick more clay outen you in a minute than you can eat in a month, you durn'd little, dirt-eatin' deer face." Clay-eating was a malady of some lower-class whites, which was often used to characterize them as degenerate.

Many of the themes recorded by these humorists had ancient roots and were not distinctly or provincially Southern. The motifs of old Southwestern yarns were similar to folklore in many parts of the world and were the common possession of illiterate folk who transferred culture orally. The Grimm brothers recorded similar tales in Germany during the early nineteenth century. In non-American folklore as well as in the published humor of the antebellum South, there were tales concerning the origin of races, animals that were humanlike, and mythical beasts. Southwestern humor contained more than its share of giants, giantesses, dwarfs, grotesques, and persons endowed with incredible power. Although the yarns of the Southwestern poor contained local color, specific detail, and individualized characters, the themes tied them to a more ancient folk past and spoke of the commonality of folk culture.

Davy Crockett's celebrated skill as a marksman provided the basis for classic yarns that emphasized poor white hunting abilities. In his autobiography, Crockett entertained his readers with an account of "the biggest bear that ever was seen in America." From a distance it was as large as a huge black bull. Crockett stalked it, then shot it twice in the breast from eighty yards distance. When these shots failed to bring it down, he rushed into the fray with butcher knife and tomahawk. On another hunt, his dogs stalked a bear on a moonless night and, for want of light, Crockett finally dived into a four-foot crack where the bear had taken refuge, felt along the animal's rump until he reached the shoulder, then plunged his butcher knife into its heart.

The folk tradition surrounding Mike Fink, who lived from 1770 to 1823, also emphasized qualities of marksmanship and violent temper. Fink slew Indians at the age of seventeen, then became a keelboatman on the Ohio and Mississippi rivers. His marksmanship was as legendary as his brawls. To test their friendship, Mike and his compatriots took turns shooting at full cups of whiskey that were placed on their heads.

The legends related by poor white storytellers concerning Crockett and Fink served the same literary function as folk architecture and crafts. They celebrated virtues necessary for survival among a people heavily dependent on hunting. They enlivened drab lives with stories of superhuman exploits.

Exaggeration was a common tool of Southern storytellers, as were grotesque characters such as Longstreet's Ransy Sniffle. Baptist preacher Harden E. Taliaferro records many stories from the Blue Ridge Mountains of North Carolina about fanciful and fearsome beasts. Uncle Davy Lane, a liar of no small ability, told of a ninety-foot tapeworm that was extracted from the gullet of gluttonous Sallie Pettigrew.

Many of the fairy tales told to antebellum poor white children obviously dated from an earlier time. They survived as the Jack Tales, preserved in purest form in the North Carolina mountains where poverty and isolation minimized the eroding effects of literacy and the outside world. "Jack and the Beanstalk" was a popular Southern version of the British story "The Boy Steals the Giant's Treasure."

Poor people were the major repository of American folklore. In the South, strong family ties, poverty, isolation, and hostility to outsiders kept oral traditions unchanged over the years; as a consequence, poor whites retained songs, superstitions, ghost stories, and tall tales long after they disappeared among the planter and yeoman classes. His folklore reflected the poor white's love of the physical, his repetition, and his imagination.

The primary objective of the storyteller was entertainment; truthfulness was of secondary importance. "The Arkansas Traveler," a story widely related in the South, incorporated the best frontier wisecrack and was circulated in many versions. The traveler stopped at a squatter's cabin to ask directions of its inhabitant who was perched atop a whiskey barrel playing a fiddle:

TRAVELER: Hello, stranger.
SQUATTER: Hello, yourself.
TRAVELER: Can I get to stay all night with you?
SQUATTER: You can git to go to hell.
TRAVELER: Have you got any spirits here?
SQUATTER: Lots of 'em. Sal saw one last night by that ole holler gum, and it nearly skeered her to death.
TRAVELER: You mistake my meaning; have you any liquor?
SQUATTER: Had some yesterday, but Ole Bose he got in and lapped al uv it outin the pot.
TRAVELER: You don't understand me. I don't mean pot liquor. I'm wet and cold, and want some whiskey. Have you got any?
SQUATTER: Oh, yes—I drank the last this morning.[4]

Some folklorists reasoned that poor whites yearned for important accomplishments, and when denied this, they obtained vicarious excitement through folklore. Whatever the explanation, the fact remains that the region's poor maintained a rich oral tradition long after it declined among other Southern classes.

In the same way that common whites adapted classic folk motifs to local characters and situations, they altered European music and religion to fit their own needs. Music, both religious and secular, assumed major importance among Southern common folk. Sacred Harp or fasola singing originated in New England before the American Revolution where individualistic Baptists tried to disassociate themselves from

Mrs. Powell, a quilt maker, Chilton County, Alabama, 1976. (*J. Mark Gooch*)

Homer Rigsby, a basket maker, Blount County, Alabama, 1976. (*J. Mark Gooch*)

Rev. B. F. Goode, a blacksmith, Alabama, 1976. (*J. Mark Gooch*)

A blacksmith Cecil Horne and his wife with their grandchildren, Alabama, 1976. (*J. Mark Gooch*)

A weaver at his loom in Tennessee, around 1930. (*Carter D. Poland. Auburn University Archives*)

A man spins thread while his daughter-in-law cards wool in a Tennessee mountain cabin. (*Carter C. Poland. Auburn University Archives*)

the older established denominations. Part of their disassociation included rejecting the songs of the established churches. In time, they developed their own body of songs. Rural New England Baptists collected these hymns, which were published in books without tunes. The preacher "lined out" or said the words of the hymn and "hist" or hissed the tune.

As Baptists followed the western valleys into the southern Piedmont and mountains, they brought their music with them. In isolated hamlets and rural communities of the southern Highlands—especially in Virginia, North Carolina, Kentucky, Tennessee, Alabama, and Georgia—this musical idiom still survived in the twentieth century. Congregations were taught to sing by note, but the notes were not the symbols current in Europe. Instead they substituted the initial letters of the four syllables *fa sol la mi,* which were placed on the five lines of the staff and in the spaces between. Each note had its own shape—circle, triangle, square—hence the name shape-note music. In springtime after crops were planted, a teacher visited the community where he would conduct a singing school in a local church, usually Primitive Baptist. Pupils were taught the notes after which they sang a tune, using the name of the notes, part by part and time after time. After it was thoroughly learned, they would substitute words for notes. Higher-voiced males sang the lead or melody line ("air"), deep-voiced males the bass, and females the "counter" (a type of tenor). Everybody beat time up and down with the right hand while singing. Singing schools lasted for a week or two, generally with a three-hour session each day.

Fasola music and the singing school slowly died in New England. Economic prosperity, European musical influences, and the growth of cities helped create a society which viewed such music as naive. But the poverty and isolation of the southern Highlands kept the idiom alive there. What survived among the South's common folk was more than merely unusual musical lyrics. It was a treasure of ancient melodies borrowed from England, Scotland, Ireland, and Wales. Most of the tunes had a secular origin; many in fact originally were set to bawdy lyrics. Celtic dance tunes became the setting for sacred texts because the fasola folk appreciated lively music, even that conceived in the devil's realm. When accompanied by the fiddle and secular dancing, the tunes were taboo; but they were too fine to ignore when the mere substitution of religious lyrics made them acceptable.

Folk music also influenced secular society. Through the efforts of Francis James Child and Cecil Sharp, the rich heritage of folk balladry has been reconstructed during the past hundred years. Child, the son of a New England sailmaker, traveled to Germany following his graduation from Harvard College in 1846. There he came into contact with the Grimm brothers, whose pioneer work in philology and comparative literature provided a method for reconstructing the past of common people. Between 1857 and 1900 Child published an impressive series of articles and books on ancient British and Scottish ballads, never dreaming that the most fertile area for retrieving such material was the remote fastness of Appalachia.

Ironically, Englishman Cecil Sharp, assisted by Olive Dame Campbell, discovered the link between Southern mountain whites and the nearly moribund English ballad. Mrs. Campbell, whose husband John C. Campbell served as director of the Southern Highland Division of the Russell Sage Foundation, traveled with her husband to remote schools in the southern Highlands. Wafting across the isolated hollows were melodies that were unfamiliar to her and wholly incongruous with the lives of the people who sang them.

Kate Thomas in remote St. Helen's, Lee County, Kentucky, sang about "The Death of Queen Jane":

> Queen Jane was in labor
> Six weeks and some more;
> The women grew wearied,
> And the mid-wife gave oer.
>
> . . . . .
>
> King Henry was sent for
> On horse-back and speed;
> King Henry he reached her
> In the hour of her need.
>
> . . . . .

O Henry, kind Henry,
Pray listen to me,
And pierce my right side open
And save my baby.

. . . . .

O no, said King Henry,
That never could be,
I would lose my sweet flower
To save my baby.

. . . . .

Queen Jane she turned over
And fell in a swound,
And her side was pierced open
And the baby was found.

. . . . .

King Henry he wept
Till his hands was wrung sore.
The flower of England
Will flourish no more.[5]

The lyrics told of proud ladies "a-dancing at the ball," of lily-white robes, of gowns of silk and castles in fair Scotland, of unrequited love and regicide, of "Lord Randal," "Sir Lionel," "Fair Annie," "Lord Lovel," "Barbara Allen," "In Seaport Town," and "The Banks of Sweet Dundee."

By 1909 Mrs. Campbell had collected seventy ballads and realized that the music had a genesis different from the songs of her own childhood. She contacted Cecil Sharp who had come to America on a lecture tour during the First World War, and the two of them collaborated to edit *English Folk Songs From The Southern Highlands* (1917).

Sharp collected some five thousand variants of songs and ballads before his death. He brought his trained musician's ear to the southern Appalachians, but divested himself of preconceived notions about musical literacy. Then he carefully recorded the traditional singing, both word and tune, without reference to any written score. These ballads had been transmitted orally since the eighteenth century from one generation of illiterate white mountain people to another until finally written down by Sharp. The lyric spoke of an older and, in some ways, a richer culture. The unusual tunes and rhythms, which first had enthralled Olive Campbell, had originated in the ancient modal scales of preharmonic music, the predecessors of the modern major and minor scales. The dialect lyrics, which were so often richer than the language of modern America, were matched by tunes that were born in a lost age of melodic excellence. It was among poor mountain whites, bypassed by progress, that this striking legacy prevailed in the years following the American Revolution.

Just as poor whites altered lyric to fit their own needs, they also modified religion. Fair appraisal of folk Christianity is made more difficult by its emotionalism, simplistic theology, and sectarianism, which so exactly fit the negative stereotype of Southern poor whites. With rare exceptions, few scholars have expressed sympathy for the Christianity of the South's poor. Yet, no one interested in the poor people of the nation's Bible Belt can ignore it.

The most famous incident in the forging of the Southern evangelical mind occurred at Cane Ridge, Kentucky, in August 1801. Following a month of publicity, a throng variously estimated from 12,000 to 25,000 gathered on a green hillside to hear a thunderous cascade of sermons, hymns, and mournful conversions. Dozens of Presbyterian, Methodist, and Baptist ministers proclaimed an emotional gospel shorn of theology but heavy with the demand for repentance. Many sinners were so overcome with guilt and remorse that they collapsed. Others were caught up in spontaneous exercises: some fell down, others rolled, jerked, barked, danced, laughed, and sang. Emotional expressions of conversion were much publicized and were employed to discredit the great revivals of the early nineteenth century, though such excesses were seldom an important part of the camp-meeting era.

Explanations for the Cane Ridge phenomenon are plentiful: the loneliness of thinly settled pioneer families, the weakness of institutional Christianity, and the harsh physical quality of life. At a deeper psychological level, Cane Ridge was an emotional catharsis for a people trapped by a hard, bitter, monotonous life. The nearness of death, the absence of law and order, and the lack of educational institutions created a population that was socially and emotionally starved. By exclusively focusing on the social function, however, some have dismissed camp-meeting Christianity with the flippant irrelevancy so often applied to the youthful courting that went on at such affairs: "more souls were made than saved."

Several recent interpretations of the camp meetings have provided an abstract explanation of the Great Revival. They focused on the common people's concept of the sovereignty of God and their total cosmology. God controlled minutely the entire operation of the universe. Everything had meaning, even the poverty and desolation of their lives, and God ultimately would turn all things to his glory and purpose. God's ultimate triumph through Christ's return stood at the center of their theological system. One sign of his imminent return was a widespread religious reawakening.

Even the songs and structure of the camp-meeting service represented one way that a frontiersman could achieve a coherent view of himself and his place in the world. The religious symbols of the camp meetings—the lyrics of the fasola hymns, the role of women in the service, the demonstration of emotion, and the conversion act itself—differed in significant ways from traditional mainline Protestantism, combining ideas from different Protestant groups with attitudes unique to the South.

Important to the poor was a sense of eternal community that gave each person a new way of looking at himself and the world. They drew strength from each other in order to confront their calamities:

> O come, and join our pilgrim band,
> Our toils and triumphs share;
> We soon shall reach the promised land,
> And rest forever there.

Camp-meeting revivalism and the sects that prospered through its use appealed most to those whites who stood outside the political and economic mainstream. Both yeomen and poor whites attended, but the lack of economic and social mobility among the poor was the key to understanding revivalistic appeal. Within the sects, members could achieve some measure of control over their lives and some degree of status. Since many preachers worked in the fields and preached only as an avocation, an illiterate farmer called by God to preach the gospel could obtain self-respect. Religion also offered an opportunity for the individualistic Southerner to control his own life, for conversion required his own conscious, affirmative act. The unpredictable life of the poor lost some of its terror when they were assured of salvation, a doctrine that was the main theme of their hymns.

World-rejection was another major element of the antebellum frontier conversion experience. The inability of a poor person to realize a better life, his frustration at trying to understand the causes of his poverty, did not result in the emergence of concrete villains to blame for his plight. He struggled in a world generally unfavorable to him, his life governed by hostile forces which he neither understood nor controlled. Conversion allowed him to enter another world that operated on two levels. On the first, that other world was a "heaven" that someday would bring relief from all his troubles; but this was no escapist mentality ("pie-in-the-sky-by-and-by"). Heaven contrasted to the hopelessness of this world. The "Canaan" imagery so common in his hymnology referred not only to heaven, but also to his sense of unity as a people beset by trouble and finding strength to cope in their common humanity. On this level, evangelical religion served him mightily in the present. People who stood outside the major political and economic processes gained a measure of control over their lives. It mitigated the violence, isolation, and instability of the Southern frontier. They were not degenerate, no matter how poor. They were not without control of their own lives, no matter how powerless. They were immortal, people for whom the Son of God had died.

Many revival evangelists knew all this. They understood the poverty and low social status of their communicants, and generally shared their plight. They used the camp meeting as a forum to repudiate the attitude of moral superiority assumed by more affluent Christians, and to attack the sins—horseracing, theater, gambling, dancing—fashionable among the planter elite; but because the sociological implications of their message were not translated into political action, their religion was considered exclusively otherworldly.

The sectarian divisions that separated antebellum poor whites from their more affluent brothers-in-Christ developed from different economic interests as well as from geographical and theological conflicts. After 1800 lower-class whites could be found predominantly among Methodist, Cumberland Presbyterian, Disciples of Christ, Missionary and Primitive Baptist congregations.

Camp-meeting revivalism represented one stream of poor white religious experience that was common to all areas of the Southern frontier; the antimission movement was another approach to the problems of life and geographically was confined mainly to the mountain regions. It arose primarily among rural Southerners who were economically insecure. The movement drew heavily upon Calvinist theology to conclude that those whom God would save were predestined to that fate, and the puny efforts of man could not alter divine intent. Consequently, it opposed camp meetings, missionary and tract societies, Sunday schools, Bible societies, denominational colleges and seminaries, and educated pastors. Such sentiments were expressed most consistently by Primitive Baptists, but the Disciples of Christ and Cumberland Presbyterians were influenced strongly by their ideas. Oftentimes the antimissionists rejected church discipline on the question of drinking liquor, considering temperance pledges unscriptural. Their religious positions corresponded to their secular notions of individualism, anti-intellectualism, and legalism.

The blossoming mission movement of the early nineteenth century, marked most notably by the formation of the American Missionary Society, contained sectional implications: most missionaries were Northerners, and missionary agencies depended heavily on religious philanthropy generated by Yankee commercial life. Well-educated Northern missionaries who worked with poor whites frequently moralized. They expressed contempt for the ignorance, provincialism, backwardness, and presumed irreligion of common whites. Although only about one-twelfth of all Southerners were churchgoers in 1829, the common folk resented the implications of missionary condescension. They thought of themselves as religious people, albeit not church-goers, and rejected attempts to convert them to a new church polity.

From this nontheological perspective, the antimission movement reflected class as well as sectional feelings. It was an expression of a deep-seated cleavage between the folk culture of poor and wealthier classes. It was consistent for Jacksonian poor whites who objected to the Bank of the United States and the Eastern financial establishment also to resent the well-educated Eastern missionaries. Poor whites who lived in mountainous regions were the most vigorous antimissionists. Within the South, support for the Missionary Baptists and their institutions—colleges, seminaries, religious instruction for white and black, mission and temperance societies—was strongest in towns and among planters and more affluent yeomen, especially those who lived in the rich coastal plain. The antimission movement, which resulted in a century-long struggle between antimissionary groups and their more affluent brethren, represented a persistent Southern struggle to preserve old values in an alien, changing, self-righteous world.

The Great Revival and the antimissionary movement of the early nineteenth century played major roles in shaping the South. According to some critics these antebellum religious enthusiasms bequeathed Southern religion an unfortunate legacy of irrational emotionalism. The theological debates produced religious obscurantism, which in turn spawned schism and sectarianism. Christian otherworldliness cut the poor white off from political action, and the anti-intellectualism that it reinforced undermined support for public education and a trained clergy. Religious values contributed to the South's exaggerated individualism and resistance to change.

Such indictments of Southern folk religion, however, are much too simplistic. Barton Stone, though not a poor white himself, was the father of the Great Revival that began at Cane Ridge, Kentucky, in 1801, and which won the hearts of poor whites. Yet, Stone did not build his religious system on emotion alone. He acknowledged that "there were many eccentricities, and much fanaticism" at Cane Ridge, but he also constructed an intricate doctrinal assault on the Westminster Confession, which led to a major split in the Presbyterian Church and contributed to the creation of the Disciples of Christ.

The poor white cosmology was not unlike that of the ancient Jews who described events in terms of primary and not secondary causes. As a people who lived in close proximity to the land and nature for longer than most Americans, poor whites were less isolated from the capriciousness of weather and geography. They knew that rain came from clouds, but they prayed mightily to God who brought the showers or halted the storms. God/fate were primary to their lives, and they seldom bothered with secondary concerns.

Poor white religion was a realistic attempt to deal with their isolation and powerlessness. Through these values, they also dealt with eternal questions of individual worth and human meaning. More affluent, better-educated people explained the search for meaning in more sophisticated theological terms, perhaps with fewer personal eccentricities; but their search was no more serious, nor was it more successful in establishing their own sense of worth. Folk religion helped bring order and stability to the frontier. It offered hope, purpose, and a sense of community. Folk culture, with religion providing a critical cement, endured longer in the South than elsewhere, and this culture preserved a quality in interpersonal relationships that soon became a casualty of the industrial revolution north of the Mason-Dixon line.

Folk religion, which emphasized individual and provincial attachments, reached beyond these limiting loyalties to help form a folk culture that was distinctive. A sense of belonging to a group emerged not from smothering provincial loyalties, but from deep commitment to local values—community, family, religion. A people whose religion stressed individuals, whose outlook and folk heroes were provincial, whose aversion to abstraction was supposedly axiomatic, produced and sustained a Southern folk culture that, for all its failures, exhibited a "relatedness and meaning" that the larger American culture was rapidly losing.

CHAPTER THREE

"LINT HEADS" AND "DIGGERS"
The Forgotten People of
the New South
1865–1920

Southern poverty became institutionalized in the postbellum years. Before the Civil War, yeoman and poor white blended into an almost indistinguishable blur, sharing common attitudes and experiences. After the war, poor whites assumed many aspects of a caste system and were increasingly identifiable within the general population. Their status became more rigid, and their alienation from the general political order more intense. There was an increase both in the numbers of white poor and in the debilitating consequences of their poverty. An economic system characterized by one-crop agriculture and poor farming methods reduced many yeomen to the status of tenants. Plagued by poor health and declining prices for their crops, farmers sought desperately for some solution to their problems. They moved off the land to work in textile mills or lumber camps. They sought villains in their real life drama, first blaming Wall Street financiers and iniquitous corporations, then bitterly turning whatever political power they gained against their black brothers-in-distress. They sought help from any source, whether Populist party, self-serving Democratic demagogues, or when desperate enough, even from the Yankee Freedmen's Bureau.

When the Civil War ended in 1865, there were many more poor whites in the South than when it had begun five years earlier. Plantation owners and once affluent merchants stood in breadlines in some Southern cities. Only pride kept others from joining them. Hard times usually fell heaviest on the poor, and the lot of common whites worsened. Many soldiers returned home in 1865 too late for a successful crop, and a drought reduced those crops that had been planted. Officials of the Freedmen's Bureau offered assistance and recorded Northern impressions of Southern poor whites. They observed women and children begging from door to door; others had not tasted meat in months; many were homeless.

The reminiscences of John William De Forest of New Haven, Connecticut, a Freedmen's Bureau agent in Greenville, South Carolina, provided a forceful description of the South's poor. He divided Greenville society into four classes: Negroes, poor whites, Unionist whites (mostly mountain people), and aristocrats. The worst off were the poor whites, whom he described as "yellow-faced" with "tallow complexions"; they were "gaunt and ragged, ungainly, stooping and clumsy in build, slouching forward."

De Forest confirmed most stereotypes of antebellum Northern travelers. Poor whites lacked ambition; they were violent, sexually promiscuous people who did not respect human life. On one occasion two women and a young girl entered his office. One of the women, in "that dull, sour, dogged tone of complaint which seems to be the natural utterance of the low-down people," complained that "my man has run me off." The man had refused to marry her because he was married already; but he had given her a ninety-year "contract" in writing, and she insisted that the federal government enforce the contract. De Forest declined to add this burden to the onerous duties of Federal Reconstruction.

Wartime devastation did change many notions concerning the proper role of government toward the public welfare and thus affected poor whites. Before the war, the South's political leadership had considered welfare a private matter. But by December 1865, five hundred thousand white indigents faced starvation, forcing some state governments to provide assistance. The South Carolina state legislature in 1866 issued three hundred thousand dollars in state bonds to purchase corn for the destitute. Both human compassion and a desire to unify whites in the face of imminent Federal Reconstruction motivated state officials, but still the relief was welcomed.

The major help came from the Bureau of Refugees, Freedmen, and Abandoned Lands, which was created by Congress in March 1865, to assist all impoverished persons regardless of race. During the first three years of its existence the bureau issued approximately 18,300,000 rations, of which 5,230,000 were dispersed to whites. By 1867, forty-six bureau hospitals served whites as well as blacks, and bureau schools were opened to both races. Tragically, many poor whites rejected such efforts as "nigger programs" and thereby damned themselves to disease, ignorance, and poverty. Few whites attended free schools created by the bureau, thus setting a precedent for later generations of poor whites who would opt for illiteracy over integration.

Although Southerners in the future would condemn Reconstruction as a radical regime dominated by Yankee opportunists, Southern traitors, and ignorant blacks, the brief era did inaugurate a general program of public welfare. Winning acceptance for these programs was not easy considering the racial views of the South's people. Most whites pridefully proclaimed Caucasian superiority, although economic wretchedness gave their boasts a hollow ring. Despite their biracial composition, the new Republican Reconstruction legislatures elected after 1866 demonstrated more interest in the plight of the white poor than the planter regimes that had preceded them. They created public schools for both races, which were usually segregated in order to make them acceptable to race-conscious whites. Most Reconstruction state governments also created boards of public charity to provide welfare for the poor. Public health boards were established to control epidemics. The governments of Alabama and Texas built poorhouses for indigents.

Racial consciousness in the Reconstruction South assured poor white rejection of such programs. Some accepted Freedmen's Bureau rations to prevent starvation, but no lesser crisis than hunger could drive them to share aid offered to blacks. They resented Republican control and black enfranchisement, and they generally sided with their race against what otherwise would have been class interests common to themselves and poor blacks. Often their racism was expressed in Ku Klux Klan style violence, which was attributed frequently to "poor young men."

With the reestablishment of Southern white state governments (called Bourbon or Redeemer) in the 1870s, political leadership fell into the hands of an amalgam of old and new aristocrats. Some came from the landed elite, but many more were New South industrialists: merchants, textile mill owners, railroad attorneys, bankers, mine owners. They urged common folk to ignore class issues so as to insure white political control. They warned that if whites split over political or economic matters, blacks would hold the balance of power and would restore Negro rule. So, conservative political hegemony was established partly as a result of the conscious choice of poor whites that race mattered more than class.

Of course, the stereotype of the solid Democratic South has been overly simplified. Disagreement among whites never disappeared. The myth that the New South was a one-party conservative monolith obscured the presence of a much more egalitarian and divisive South. Many factors contributed to this division: socioeconomic differences within the region, a democratic ideology common to many non-Southerners, and the nation's political alignment. In national elections, most white Southerners voted Democratic; but state politics presented a different picture. Although the aristocracy exercised disproportionate influence because of the sense of white unity forged by the Civil War and Reconstruction, independent parties challenged Democratic hegemony between 1870 and 1900. They were called by many names—Readjusters, the People's Anti-Bourbon party, the Greenback-Labor party, Jeffersonian Democrats, Populists—but whatever their name they challenged conservative Democrats. At one level their protest was a defense of rural values against the encroachments of mercantile/industrial American society. More importantly, the revolt arose among white farmers driven to desperation by prolonged agricultural depression and the indifference of conservative Democratic governments.

The first clue to the nature of the new Redeemer order appeared in the form of reduced state budgets for public programs. Such projects during the Reconstruction era had been funded by property taxes, falling heaviest on landowners and industrialists. Upon gaining control of state government, these classes predictably dismantled welfare programs. The average public school term declined, with a resulting rise in white illiteracy; welfare expenditures of all types fell. Since the county was the basic political unit in the South, most welfare was administered at this level. Following Reconstruction the counties adopted three basic methods of dealing with the poor: the almshouse; public funds awarded to families; and leasing. In the last of these, indigent persons could be leased to the highest bidder for a stipulated time. Usually leasing was limited to blacks, although in North Carolina some whites also fell victim. These methods were modified after 1900 by progressive political legislation, but administration of state welfare monies remained in the hands of county governments in most states until the 1930s.

Although the economic condition of poor whites did not improve quantitatively during the years of Redeemer rule, they were absorbed into the economic system. Before the Civil War, their economic isolation was as complete as their geographical seclusion. Subsistence agriculture was the chief occupation and they did not produce much for the market. Between 1865 and 1900, they gradually entered the economic system as industrial wage earners or tenant farmers. This assimilation did not bring prosperity, but at least the wage and tenant system provided a place for poor whites within prevailing economic institutions.

The extent of white poverty increased in the late nineteenth century, the numbers augmented by thousands of former yeomen whose condition was steadily worsening. Although some antebellum small farmers had become prosperous landowners or merchants, thousands more were descending into the ranks of tenant farmers, textile mill workers, or miners.

The Southern Poor White Caste

Despite the absence of a distinctive race, skin color, or laws, poor whites assumed most of the aspects of a separate caste. They shared unequally in privileges and opportunities. They infrequently married yeomen or planters. Their integration into the economic system did not allow them access into middle and upper classes.

The postwar Southern caste system has been described in various ways, but most agree concerning the rigidness of class parameters and the difficulty of escaping from the bottom level. The post-Reconstruction alliance of whites that restored Caucasian hegemony created a system of control that caused the economic, political, and social status of poor whites to deteriorate. The poor were gradually excluded from the political process by means of the poll tax and literacy tests. County government became the domain of a small but powerful elite, which used its institutions to dominate the poor of both races who were divided by racial animosity. Institutions such as schools and county government, including the critical office of sheriff, were controlled by middle and upper classes and were unresponsive to poor whites.

Even churches became polarized along class lines. Caste differentiation helps explain the increasing appeal of a variety of Baptist sects to poor whites. Also, after 1900 Pentecostal and Holiness churches became increasingly attractive to lower-class folk.

There were many causes of increased class rigidity: inadequate transportation, one-crop agriculture, poor farming techniques, absence of credit and banking facilities, illiteracy, and poor health. The South had not developed an adequate transportation system, and farmers could not get to towns where more options might be available for shopping, credit, and schooling, or where they could market their crops more profitably. So, they relied on the country store owner who performed critical functions of providing credit, marketing crops, and supplying goods. The lack of transportation helped enslave the farmer to nonperishable farm products (cotton, tobacco, sugar cane), which could be hauled in crude wagons over miserable roads without danger to the crop, then stored for long periods of time.

Although tradition and ignorance imposed a system of one-crop agriculture, that alone did not explain the dominance of cotton and tobacco among poor farmers. Merely dethroning King Cotton would not save the farmer; he needed some economic alternative. Agricultural diversification had to await selective breeding of livestock, cheap fertilizers, new products, and expanded markets. The hardware catalogues, which were circulated in the South between 1865 and 1900, demonstrated the Southern farmer's reliance on essentially the same agricultural technology as before the war. Not until the dual revolutions of the tractor, which first affected the South in the 1920s, and the cotton picker, which arrived mainly in the 1940s, did the primitive horse, mule, and plow era give way to modern farming. No doubt traditionalism locked poor whites into agricultural backwardness; but even had they desired alternatives, the cost would have been beyond their reach.

Poor farming methods helped account for the hopelessness of the poor. Their farming techniques exhausted the soil, and the fertility of their land declined. A tradition of unfenced free grazing inhibited selective breeding of livestock.

Other economic factors were less susceptible to their control. Competition from abroad conspired with the Southerner's obsession with cotton to drive the price per bale steadily lower. A bale of cotton brought $83.38 at inflated 1865 prices; by 1866 the price had fallen to $43.60; in the 1890s a bale brought less than $30.00.

Health was also a factor in class rigidity. A diet that lacked fresh fruits and vegetables left farmers malnourished. Nutritional ailments, malaria, hookworm, and lack of medical and dental care took a huge toll on the energy of farmers.

The unique malady of poor whites, and one which figures large in the stereotype of the class, was clay-eating. Antebellum travel accounts first designated poor whites living in the barren areas of the Southeastern states as "clay-eaters." Southwestern humorists used the practice as a stock characteristic of the Ransy Sniffle type characters. According to their accounts, common whites took the clay directly from the ground or from between the logs of their cabins. People whose characters were described as ignorant, shiftless, and morally degraded were said to have bodies that were "sickly, sallow, unnatural . . ."

Clay-eating, technically called geophagy, was mentioned by physicians during the antebellum period. Until the early 1900s it was assumed that clay-eating was caused by hookworm. But the campaign to eradicate hookworm launched by the Rockefeller Commission in 1909 did not eliminate clay-eating. A new phase of medical research began in 1941 when it was discovered that the practice persisted among poor children in rural Mississippi. In recent years a survey of the outpatients at the Obstetrics-Gynecology Clinic at Duke Medical Center in North Carolina indicated that approximately one quarter were clay-eaters. Years after successful hookworm eradication, clay-eating continued among the poor of both sexes and races in the South.

Recent research indicates that although the practice was widespread, many clay-eaters suffered no apparent ill effects; the listlessness and sallow complexions long associated with the clay-eater were often absent. The practice thrived among poor people with a family history of pica (an abnormal craving for certain unnatural foods, especially during pregnancy or hysteria). The habit was deep-rooted in a culture of poverty, ignorance, and superstition. Many men believed that eating clay increased sexual prowess, and some females claimed that eating clay helped pregnant women to have an easy delivery. The bitter-sour taste of some clays stimulated the appetite and soon became a pre-meal habit. There is no medical evidence to support the traditional opinion that the practice arose from vitamin or mineral deficiencies, although this possibility is still under investigation.

Other dietary and health problems constituted an immediate hazard. Pellagra, caused by a deficiency of nicotinic acid and characterized by gastrointestinal disorders, drained the energy of the lower class. Hookworms invaded through the bare feet, infested the small intestine, and resulted in anemia, fever, weakness, and abdominal pain. Such diseases could not be treated professionally because of the absence of clinics, physicians, and hospitals. The rural poor frequently had only two medical choices: treat themselves or do without. To compensate for the absence of professional care, poor folk passed along orally from generation to generation a store of folk medicine that combined both superstition and empirical wisdom. Frequently such remedies were without medical validity, but others demonstrated that the folk mind was a remarkable repository of wisdom founded on generations of trial-and-error experimentation.

The woman was the chief transmitter of this medical folk wisdom, perhaps due to her role as midwife and nurse. The state of her art was primitive as demonstrated by the remedies of Jessie Thrasher of McCalla, Alabama, who was typical of many folk doctors who retained the medical lore of an earlier age. She described the cure for a child's colic: "Well, back in the olden days they took asafetida (gum resin) and whiskey and mixed it together, a certain amount of each; then when the baby had the colic they would shake that up and would give a drop per pound, for each pound the baby weighed." A poultice made from red clay and vinegar was wrapped around a sprained ankle. "Night sweats" could be cured with tea made from white oak bark. The bark was placed in boiling water and steeped for twenty minutes and then given to drink. Medicinal tea could be brewed also from sage or strawberry leaves. For laxatives Aunt Jessie remembered:

> They would gather a grass that they called blue grass in the spring of the year. Each and anyone had to take a dose to purify their blood and cleanse their body and they would . . . gather the blue grass and put it on and boil it like we would our tea. Then they would put a certain amount of sugar or syrup in it to sweeten it, and it was a real good laxative. After you had taken the tea and was over it you really had an appetite. You could eat anything they put before you.[1]

Such medical remedies were not unlike the houses built from whatever materials their physical environment provided. Without money for formal medical care, they turned to nature. Trial and error finally produced results that reduced pain or at least reassured them psychologically. Despite all their efforts and folk wisdom, poor health remained

Tennessee cabin, early twentieth century. (*Carter D. Poland. Auburn University Archives*)

Cane Ridge Church in Kentucky, where the "Great Revival" began in August 1801.

Dogtrot cabin in South Alabama, 1975. (*Wayne Flynt*)

Mine camp, Birmingham, Alabama, early twentieth century.
(*Birmingham Public Library*)

a factor in the poverty of the bottom class.

Some social scientists argue that the South never had a caste system. Perhaps enough mobility did exist to make this an arguable point. But certainly the rigid social and economic distinction of poor whites marked them as a distinct group. The causes of their plight were partly of their own making, but also partly beyond their control. Most lived on farms, isolated, beyond institutional assistance; they were often ill and captives of a prescientific medical system. Together with their one-crop agriculture, poor farming methods, and international economic competition, they became shackled to a way of life significantly different from their white fellows of the "better" classes.

Tenants and Sharecroppers

The predominant institutional expression of the caste system was farm tenancy. Although some of the South's white poor lived in cities and engaged in industrial occupations before 1920, most dwelt in rural areas and farmed. When the Bureau of Census for the first time investigated the number of landless Southern farmers in 1880, it discovered that tenants operated 36.2 percent of all Southern farms. By 1920 the figure had risen to 49.2 percent. Furthermore, white tenants outnumbered black ones, although a higher percentage of black farmers were tenants. The increase in white farm tenancy may have been the most striking economic trend in an era that saw the South's economy ostensibly *yankeeized* and modernized.

The dominant causes of tenant farming are well known: lack of credit in a region with few banks, poor transportation, and the fear of a labor shortage following the abolition of slavery. Plantations remained after 1865, but in theory they were divided into individual farms worked by families who lived in dogtrot or shotgun houses. Two major subtypes of renters became blended by the single designation *tenant farmer*. The sharecropper was most typical of the system as a whole, but relatively more poor blacks than whites were croppers. The owner usually supplied the cropper with mules, implements, seed, fertilizer, land, and a house. Oral agreements between landowner and cropper determined the kind of crop and the quantity to be planted. When the crop was harvested in the fall, it was usually divided equally. The landowner tended to exercise much more supervision over croppers than over tenants, perhaps because they were poorer.

The tenant renter, the second subtype, supplied his own mules and implements in addition to most of his seed and fertilizer. Tenants might pay rent in one of several ways. A cash tenant paid a stipulated amount for a year's rent. "Standing rent" was a term applied to a tenant who paid a specified amount of his produce annually. Most frequently, the tenant agreed to give the landowner one-third of his crop in payment. Tenants enjoyed a higher economic status than croppers, but were not necessarily more productive farmers. The tenant system spread partly as a result of a management decision by the landowner who observed that croppers made better use of stock and equipment when they owned it. So, owners arranged for croppers to buy animals and implements on time, or they took a larger share of the crop to pay for them.

Under the tenant system the owner and tenant decided jointly what to produce, but the landowner generally preferred that the renter produce a staple item that could be marketed easily. In most sections of the South, cotton was the obvious preference. In attempting to produce as large a cash crop as possible, the tenant ignored food crops and planted no more than necessary to feed his family. Every additional inch of his thirty- or forty-acre patch was devoted to cotton. The steady decline of cotton prices took an ever-larger toll in payment for this policy. In good years, the tenant might make ten to fifteen bales, and his annual income would soar to seven or eight hundred dollars. Depression decades such as the 1890s brought five cent per pound cotton and annual incomes dropped to below a hundred dollars.

Even had he produced grains or other crops his condition would not have improved significantly. The productivity of the tenant farmer was not comparable to the effort he expended toiling on the land regardless of his crop. No generalization about his work is adequate because success depended on each person's industry, agricultural techniques, the type of soil he farmed, the size of the tenant's family, weather conditions, and a dozen other variables. One agricultural historian ranked postbellum agricultural productivity with the white cotton farmer at the top, the black cotton farmer next, and black noncotton farmers third; at the bottom were white noncotton farmers. The low productivity of white noncotton farmers was due to their antebellum heritage, which left them living on the worst land— worn-out flatland and the Appalachian slopes. Even though black tenants were treated worse than their white counterparts by white landowners, they were often more productive farmers. Although the financial condition of white tenants might not have improved had they diversified, the production of more vegetables and fruits certainly would have improved their diet and health.

Rarely did any tenant, regardless of color, realize a cash profit at the year's end. He relied on a local merchant for the necessities that he could not raise or make. Merchants took high risks by extending credit to tenants and charged accordingly. When "settling up" time came in the fall, the tenant's share of the crop usually did little more than cover his debt.

Urbanization and Industrialization of Poor Whites

The grinding poverty of the tenant system forced many off the land in the years following the Civil War. Spokesmen for the new industrial order promised them a better life in the mill towns and mining camps springing up amidst the cotton rows and clay hills of the Piedmont and southern Highlands. These secular missionaries to the tenants made many converts, and by the tens of thousands poor whites left the unequal struggle on the land for the factory's whirling spindles and the lonely blackness of the mine. The population of the South in 1860 was 93 percent rural; only 63 urban areas of more than 2,500 inhabitants lay between the Potomac River and Texas. By 1930 there were 730 such cities and towns in the same area. In 1880 less than eight percent of America's manufacturing wage earners lived in the South; by 1939, more than seventeen percent resided in the region.

Changes did occur in the years following the Civil War, but the magnitude of these changes must not be exaggerated. There was no more a New South economically than there was in attitudes toward blacks; farming and white supremacy reigned supreme. Yet, industry began to make inroads into the agrarian way of life. Between 1880 and 1900, the number of wage earners and the value of their products tripled. The cigarette machine revolutionized the South's tobacco industry. Iron and steel production and coal mining dominated the economics within an arc sweeping south from the corners of Kentucky, Virginia, and West Virginia, across Tennessee and into northern Alabama. The decline of northern timber resources stimulated exploitation of the hardwoods of the southern Appalachians and the extensive yellow pine forests along the coast.

The new industrial base was narrow: textiles, lumber, furniture making, tobacco, coal mining, iron and steel. It was exploitive, also, leaning heavily on the region's abundant raw materials, the seemingly endless pool of poverty-stricken cheap labor, and the absence of unions and political radicalism. Conditions in the new industrial order soon caused many poor whites to doubt the wisdom of their exodus from the land.

Most of these new industries drew workers from local farms who were eager for alternative jobs promising a better life. Attracting textile mills became a secular crusade to save the South's poor whites. An evangelist in North Carolina in the late nineteenth century reportedly proclaimed: "Next to God, what this town needs is a cotton mill." In *The Wasted Land,* Gerald Johnson wrote that the textile mill movement was not a business but a social enterprise:

> Any profit that might accrue to the originators of the mill was but incidental; the main thing was the salvation of the decaying community and especially of the poor whites who were in danger of being submerged altogether ... People were urged to take stock in the mills for the town's sake, for the poor people's sake, for the South's sake, literally for God's sake.[2]

During the years after 1880 tens of thousands of tenants moved into the mill villages of the southern Piedmont. In 1860 the South counted 10,152 mill workers; in 1870, 10,173; in 1880, 16,741; in 1890,

36,415; in 1900, 97,559. The number of looms had increased from 8,789 in 1860, to 110,015 in 1900.

The route from independent farmer to mill worker was as varied as the poor folk who followed it; there was no typical pattern. But each story reflected its own human drama. Mrs. L. A. House was born in 1885 in Shelby County, Alabama, among the rolling hills of the southernmost Appalachians. Her father operated a country store and saloon and managed a charcoal pit; her mother actually earned more than her father as a seamstress specializing in making men's clothes. Her father purchased a farm with the combined family savings, but knew nothing about agriculture and lost the investment. He became a Populist in the 1890s and blamed his misfortune on President Grover Cleveland and the federal government. Mrs. House married in 1899 at the age of fourteen ("I married real young. Been married all by life") and gave birth to five children. Her husband bought a plot and they farmed until he became ill with cancer. To pay their medical bills they mortgaged their farm. When he died in 1913, Mr. House had no money or land left. She became a tenant, farming thirty acres that she rented for one hundred dollars a year. With the help of her brother and oldest son, she tried to stay on the land.

After several years' effort at subsistence agriculture, she left her children in the care of relatives and went into the little town of Sylacauga where she found employment at B. B. Comer's textile mill working seventy-two hours a week for nine dollars. She quit in the springtime and went back to the farm to try a last crop, but she was no more successful than before. In the early 1920s she deserted the land and the country Methodist Church she loved and brought her family into the mill village permanently. She acknowledged that the mill work was hard, but most of the mill folk had been farmers, and textile work "was much easier than digging." She changed churches because the Methodist Church "got all the big people, you know, all the stewards and men out of the mill . . . I just liked the people better over at the other [Mignon Baptist] church. They were more like I was; the labor." She appreciated Comer's acts of kindness toward his workers, seldom felt abused, and opposed unionization of the mill workers.[3]

The textile mill was no panacea for poor whites, dispensing assistance and calamity with utter disregard for the motives of paternalistic mill owners such as Comer. Even the most charitable Southern entrepreneurs tried to make profits while rescuing poor whites from agrarian misery; and for some of them, making money clearly outweighed "the poor people's sake." Conditions in the mill villages were better than on a tenant farm but still were wretched. In the 1890s salaries in the North Carolina mills sagged to an average of fifty cents a day, and seventy-hour work weeks were common. Between 1890 and 1900, the number of laborers under the age of fifteen employed in the industry tripled to 25,000. Ninety percent of these children labored in the four leading textile states of Georgia, Alabama, and the Carolinas.

The textile mill village was similar to the antebellum plantation. It was isolated from the adjacent community, produced a single staple commodity, utilized a largely unskilled labor force, and created its own self-contained institutions. Despite these similarities, the village was different from the plantation in some critical aspects. The labor force was Caucasian in deference to the racial views of poor whites. There was no guarantee against unemployment, disability, or old age, and the occasional paternalism of an individual mill owner did not soften the total impact of the industry on the poor. Class consciousness began to grow from the moment the poor settled together in mill towns.

Historians generally have ignored the labor movement in the South. They have assumed that the South's individualism, its otherworldly religion, and its white racial solidarity made unionism impossible. Despite such assumptions, the labor movement grew in the South during the late nineteenth century. When the Knights of Labor began to decline nationally in 1886, it turned its organizational effort to the South. By the end of that year, there were some 45,700 members of the Knights in the Southern states. Southern locals embraced farmers, textile operatives, sugar cane workers, timber workers, and urban craftsmen. The membership of some locals was interracial although most blacks were organized in separate groups. The Knights effectively mobilized their urban adherents for political action, and elected mayors of Vicksburg, Mississippi; Anniston, and Selma, Alabama; and Jacksonville, Florida. Laborers and their allies elected a congressman in Virginia and 11 of 15 members of the Lynchburg city council; in Georgia, they elected several state legislators and a majority of the city officials in Macon. Their political sophistication was sufficient to enable them to forge pragmatic coalitions with black Republican leaders and middle-class white reformers.

Redeemer Democrats charged that the Knights were too radical on economic and racial issues because they sought to organize all working people and were willing to use strikes as a weapon. Despite the union's official recognition of "the civil and political equality of all men," it was hardly a radical organization. But the Knights' attempt to align poor white textile workers, farmers, and blacks in the 1880s was an important prelude to the Populist revolt of the 1890s.

During the 1890s labor unrest intensified. In north Alabama the newly formed United Mine Workers union began an organizing drive to counter falling wages. The coal mine labor force was made up of free and convict labor of both races. About thirty-five percent of the work force was drawn from native-born poor whites, nineteen percent was immigrant, and forty-seven percent black. In April 1894, some nine thousand coal miners walked off their jobs. Both sides resorted to violence in the following weeks, but despite charges that the white strikers were working with Negroes against their own race, the laborers maintained solidarity. Finally, the governor of Alabama used the state militia to break the strike. Although the union was destroyed, poor whites and blacks had worked together for common economic objectives. Furthermore, the strikers gave critical assistance to the Populist gubernatorial candidate in 1894, providing a large segment of his vote in the mining counties of north Alabama.

Labor organizations continued to grow after 1900, although race relations within the labor movement became more strained. The number of unions in Memphis, Tennessee, for instance, increased from 25 with 600 members in 1898, to 45 with 2,650 members in 1901. The segregationist racial policy of the American Federation of Labor, which led the organizing effort after 1900, caused blacks to lose skilled jobs, and immigrant labor became increasingly significant. Italian and Eastern European workers assumed many of the jobs in the Birmingham iron district and in the Appalachian coal fields. Native-born white workers often demonstrated as much antipathy toward their strange-talking, Catholic, white companions as they did toward blacks.

The most violent union activity during the period occurred among timber workers in northeastern Texas and Louisiana. In 1910 the Brotherhood of Timber Workers was organized with headquarters at Alexandria, Louisiana. Negroes composed about half the union's peak membership of 35,000, with white lumbermen and poor white farmers who lived near the lumber towns constituting the balance. A conflict with the timber companies began in 1910 which ultimately destroyed the union. By 1912 the Brotherhood was financially exhausted and its five thousand remaining members voted to join the Industrial Workers of the World, one of the nation's more radical unions. The timber workers' most violent strike occurred in Merryville, Louisiana, in February 1913, where townsmen and company guards were determined to destroy the union. Town vigilantes instituted a three-day reign of terror, destroyed the union soup kitchen, raided the union hall, and ran two-thirds of its three hundred members out of town.

Desperation drove essentially individualistic, religious people into unionism. By 1900, twenty-five percent of Alabama's textile labor force was under the age of sixteen. Illiteracy among these children, some of them as young as twelve, was three times as great as for non-working youngsters. Alabama coal miner Elmer Burton remembered Christmas singings at Gamble Mines Church just after 1900 when his mother presented him with a present of oranges or a single toy. An orange was considered a special gift because children received them only at Christmas or when sick.

Thousands of Southern workers were discovering for themselves that industry was a Frankenstein, beckoning them from a hard, monotonous life on the land with beguiling promises, then providing only more poverty amidst the choking lint of the textile mill or the unrelenting gloom of the coal mine.

The Farmers' Revolt

The growing class consciousness among poor whites found its most spectacular expression in the Farmers' Alliance and Populist party. In the late 1870s, probably 1877, Texas farmers formed the Farmers' Alliance as an educational and social organization. It spread rapidly throughout the South until it numbered three million white and one-and-a-quarter million black members by 1890. Most Alliancemen owned farms, and the Alliance did not recruit actively among poor white tenants. The poorest rural whites lacked the nominal amount of cash, a few cents a month, required to join the order. In South Carolina a survey taken in 1888 revealed that fifty-five percent of the members owned farms and thirty-one per cent were tenants. In the Southwest, tenants constituted a larger share of the membership; one Texas Alliance spokesman estimated that most Alliancemen in the Lone Star State were tenants. Initially the Alliance was primarily educational, but it turned to politics in the late 1880s, working first within the Democratic party. This effort was successful in electing politicians who were nominally associated with the Alliance; but once in office they ignored the Alliance platform, which demanded federal warehouses for storing crops and governmental loans. After failing to reform the Southern Democratic party from within, Alliance leaders formed a new party in 1891 called the Peoples or Populist party. Many middle-class farmers who had belonged to the Alliance renounced the new party, but poorer farmers welcomed it. Blacks formed an important wing of the new coalition. Although Southern Populists were not racially egalitarian, an alliance of the poor of both races seemed to offer the only realistic hope for wresting power from Democratic Redeemers. Tom Watson, Georgia Populist leader, ran for Congress backed by a coalition of poor white Democrats and poor black Republicans. "You are kept apart," he warned, "that you may be separately fleeced of your earnings."

Historians still debate whether Populism was a nostalgic last stand for an agrarian way of life, a nativist defense of fundamental Anglo-Saxon rural values, or a realistic appraisal of the inequities produced by American industrialism. Many of the issues that the Populists raised

—regulation of trusts, inflated currency, fairer treatment of labor—
were class issues and suggest the division of Southern life along socioeconomic lines. One historian of Populism in Louisiana traced the
movement to the economic conditions of poor whites between 1860
and 1890; Populism was essentially an uprising by this class. An historian of the agrarian crusade in Alabama concluded that industrial
and agricultural poverty also spawned the movement there. In South
Carolina Benjamin Tillman hitched his political career to the awakening class consciousness of white tenant farmers and textile mill workers. The Populist coalition cannot be explained entirely by class conflict; yet, this was a facet of the revolt.

Part of the historical confusion about Southern Populism resulted
from unwillingness to recognize the presence of class consciousness in
the 1880s, which already had resulted in labor organization. Although
politics revealed class conflict most clearly, it can be seen in other aspects of Southern culture including that most sacrosanct and conservative institution, the church. Among Methodists and Baptists, denominational leadership came from larger, better-educated, and more affluent churches, the First Church elite, which dominated small towns and
cities. From the pastors of such churches came convention presidents,
college officials, editors of sectarian newspapers, and the future pastors
of other First Churches. The official stance of this leadership was typi-
cally hostile to Populism. Since such social conservatism fits the image
of otherworldly evangelical Southern Christianity, it came to stereotype the entire evangelical church reaction to Populism.

Beneath this religious elite existed a subchurch dominated by poor
whites. Their uneducated preachers frequently earned a livelihood on
the land or in mill villages in the same occupations as their parishioners.
During the early 1890s the *Alabama Baptist*, state journal of the denomination, was filled with mission reports chiding churches for the
decline in offerings due to political divisions among Baptists over the
issue of Populism. Receipts declined as pastors neglected the work of
Zion to busy themselves with divisive secular politics. Acrimonious debates erupted among the pastors who argued the wisdom of a minister
entering politics. Judging by the involvements of pastors, the debate

certainly was justified: Rev. Samuel M. Adams of Bibb County served in turn as president of the Alabama Farmers' Alliance, of the Populist movement in the state, and as leader of Populists in the Alabama House of Representatives; Rev. J. M. Loftin served as an Alliance officer in Bullock County, as did Rev. John L. Stuart in Covington County; the Rev. A. J. Hearn was a fervent Populist leader in Choctaw County. In Louisiana many of the early Populist organizational meetings in the white hill counties were conducted in Primitive Baptist churches. Baptist ministers served as presidents of the Georgia Alliance and the Florida Populist party. Many of the Populist orators were ministers who brought evangelical rhetoric to the movement. They defined scripture and the mission of the church in ways that justified their attempts to reform society through political action.

The Populist revolt, rooted in increasing awareness of poor white grievances, did not win control of the South's politics, but it did deflect the Democratic party into more liberal channels. New leadership within the dominant party realized that the simplest way to absorb the Populists into the white man's party was to resolve Populist grievances. This course became even more advisable when the party replaced the caucus-controlled convention system of nominating candidates with the direct white primary. The white primary gave a critical advantage to candidates who could stir the passions of the masses. Some of these emotions grew from legitimate concerns such as Redeemer neglect of poor white farmers, child labor, and the abuses of trusts; other passions came from the darker recesses of poor whites who had been neglected and abused too long. They were angry and sought scapegoats to explain their condition. A new breed of Democratic leadership soon provided a multitude of scapegoats.

Racism and Demagoguery

The Democratic party organization was apathetic and even hostile to the interests and needs of the great mass of common people, white and black, but no effective biracial political coalition evolved from this opportunity. Instead, aspiring politicians utilized the direct primary to inflame the white masses over some grievance, real or imagined. The issues ranged from corporation control of state government to fear of Negro rapists. Once elected, the demagogues often ignored the issues they had raised and sometimes enacted extensive reform programs. Whether reformers or not, they often installed corrupt regimes, which they maintained in power by further racial and class appeals.

The era of Benjamin Tillman and Cole Blease in South Carolina offers a suggestive case study. Tillman promised help to poor farmers and mill workers in the 1890s, and they elected him governor, then United States senator. He attempted to resolve their problems while in office. After a brief interruption, Cole Blease claimed Tillman's reform mantle, taking his 1910 gubernatorial campaign to the same poor white constituency.

Both Tillman and Blease appealed to the poor white electorate. A quarter of the white population lived in the textile mill villages of South Carolina, and most remembered vividly the frustrations of the tenant farm. Sixty-three percent of the state's farms were cultivated by tenants. In the 1914 Democratic primary, 107,894 white men applied to vote, and 22,251 of them signed with a mark because they could not write. As late as 1927 the average per capita wage of a textile worker in the state was only 654 dollars per year.

Blease betrayed poor whites in office, offering them nothing more than vicious, warped racism. But a generation of well-educated, conservative Redeemers had betrayed them just as badly before Blease, ignoring the plight of the poor and damning them to illiteracy and poverty. The Columbia *State*, voice of the state's conservative "better families," editorialized on Blease: "We believe his leadership of the poor man the worst leadership the poor man could have." The editorial missed the point; Blease often provided the only voice the poor man had.

In the years from 1880 to 1920 violence spread across the South, stirred by men such as Blease. Lynchings increased as poor whites struck out at the nearest and most defenseless "villain." The typical lynch county in the South was mostly white, sparsely populated, and overwhelmingly poor. Participants in lynch mobs were generally poorly educated, unchurched, and propertyless. The harder the times, the more frequent the lynchings. The need for scapegoats in the 1890s made those depression years the heyday of extralegal violence. Between 1889 and 1899, an average of 188 lynchings occurred each year; this figure dropped to 93 between 1900 and 1909, to 62 from 1910 to 1919, and 46 between 1920 and 1924. Defenders of lynchings usually justified such actions as a defense of Southern womanhood. Yet, only one-fifth of all lynchings actually involved rape, either real or alleged. Some observers distinguished between an upper-class and a poor white lynching. The former was better planned, the method of murder less bizarre, and the lynching attracted fewer observers. Poor white mobs were less orderly, attracted more people, and sometimes engaged in additional violence against property. Propertyless members of a lynch mob in Sherman, Texas, shouted while the courthouse burned: "Let 'er burn down; the taxpayers'll put 'er back."

Economic competition provided a convenient excuse for attacks on blacks. In southwestern Mississippi small dirt farmers attempted to drive blacks away because local merchants used Negroes to work land, which they obtained by foreclosure. Many white laborers turned violent when Negro strikebreakers were imported to fill their jobs. The subculture of poor white communities tolerated violence that resulted from community consensus, and protests against it came usually from the more affluent classes.

Yet, racism and violence represented only one aspect of common white experience. These years also produced political and economic cooperation between the races within both the Knights of Labor and the Populists. Although not all whites within such organizations favored biracial politics, in a few areas such as Jefferson County, Alabama, the poor of both races fought for a better life side by side. These whites were not integrationists or advocates of social equality; but they momentarily realized that the restrictions which divided them also kept them poor, and they tried to breach such barriers. The failure of their effort, and the failure of the generation that followed them, left poor whites nearly as impoverished in 1930 as they had been in 1890.

Poor White Folk Culture

Although racism has been singled out by many social scientists for primary attention, it was only one aspect of a multifaceted folk culture. In their lore and songs, religion and superstition, poor whites accommodated the grim realities of their lives to their personal sense of meaning. Despite all their grief and misery, they retained their own notions of worth and even their humor.

Folklore was not trivial storytelling; it was life related. It revealed how poor people coped with problems. The legendary country store played a major role in the bittersweet existence of the poor. It often functioned as an extortive institution charging high prices for commodities purchased on credit. But the plain people also spent hours spinning yarns around its potbellied stove in wintertime, and many a political debate resounded among the barrels of crackers, sugar, coffee, and pickles.

Sometimes the distance from poor white to country merchant was not too great. Many stories in poor white folklore explained how illiterate merchants solved the problem of record-keeping:

> Bill Bunker who could neither read nor write did more business than any man in the horn of the moon. And . . . when a feller bought anything, he'd draw a picture of what he got. Then that's the way he kept books. And one time . . . a feller come up to pay. He had him charged with a hoop of cheese, and this feller said, "I don't owe you for no cheese; we actually sold cheese. We never bought no cheese." He said, "Well, I tell you, . . . I did buy a grindstone from you last year." "Ah," he said, "That's it, I just left out the hole in the middle for the crank."[4]

The folklore surrounding the country store constituted only one aspect of a rich oral tradition that continued from the antebellum years. Among poorly educated people, oral lore assumed a major role in the transmission of culture, and most tenant farmers received little education. As a consequence, common folk combined superstition, folk beliefs, and evangelical Christianity into a strange concoction. Witches and ghosts inhabited the same world as saints and angels. Many of the stories were the New World survivals of ancient Celtic religion, which better-educated and more affluent Americans had abandoned long before. Just as the ancient musical idiom lived on among the white poor, so did ancient superstition. Many poor folk believed that a person about to die received a sign, and folklore contains numerous examples of banshee cries or visits by a "fetch" or likeness of another person that warned of his impending death. They believed that "fetch lights" hovered over a house when someone in the family was about to die. Such beliefs had originated centuries earlier in Ireland and were still transmitted orally by believers in the South in the early twentieth century.

Poor whites were not only politically and economically powerless, they were also helpless against the whims of nature. So, they contrived a rich body of superstition to control the weather. Too much rain or not enough were equally disastrous problems and could not be left entirely to chance: "if you kill a cricket, it will rain"; "if you kill a frog, it will rain"; "if you hang a snake belly up, it will rain in three days." One study of Alabama folk belief records one hundred ninety portents and sayings about how to summon or end rain.

Wells were discovered by water witching, using a forked stick from a willow or fruit tree. Holding the prongs in both hands, or one of them between the teeth, with the branch end pointed up, a man walked toward a likely spot. If water was near, the branch turned mysteriously until it pointed straight to the spot where the well was to be placed. The harder one squeezed the stick to keep the prongs from turning, the more they moved inexorably downward.

Despite grim economic realities, poor whites did not lose the ability to laugh at themselves. Folktales provided an excellent medium for their humor. One story common to rural Southerners involved a classic mistake of identification:

> One time there was an old farmer that said he was a little hard of hearing. The truth is, he was so deef he couldn't hear it thunder. His cow had strayed off somewhere, and the old man walked all over the country asking folks if they had seen her, but they all shook their heads.

Finally, he met up with a preacher, and he says to the preacher, "Will you tell all the church folks about my cow being lost?" The preacher nodded his head to mean yes. So that night the old man went to church. He figured that when the people heard about the cow, he could maybe find out where she was saw last.

The sermon was pretty long, but the deef man set quiet till it was over. Then the preacher begun to tell the folks about a young couple that was going to get married. The fellow was a fine young man, he says. The girl was a teacher in the Sunday School, so the preacher laid it on pretty thick. He says this young lady is the cream of the crop and the flower of the flock and the pride of Durgenville, and then he says she is a fine sample of Christian womanhood, and a inspiration to young people all over the country.

The old man couldn't hear a word, but he figured the preacher was telling the people about his cow. So pretty soon he got up and hollered, "her rump's caved in, folks, and she's got one spoiled tit!"

The preacher just stood there with his mouth open, as he had forgot all about the old cow. Some of the young folks pretty near died laughing. The girl began to bawl, and the young fellow says he will kill the old bastard if it's the last thing he ever done. The meeting busted in a terrible fight, and the sheriff grabbed the deef man and run for the jailhouse. The sheriff he figured the old man better be locked up for his own good.

It was away later in the night before things quietened down. Then the preacher and some other folks come to the jail and told the sheriff how it was. So they turned the old man loose, and a fellow that worked in the bank took him out home in a buggy. Some folks say that the deef man never did get it through his head what all the trouble was about. The poor old fellow didn't come to town very often after that. He says everybody in the settlement is plumb crazy, and it ain't safe for a respectable citizen to go there nowadays.[5]

Occasionally religious folklore contained elements of class division. A story entitled "Adam and Eve" emphasized the chasm between well-educated ministers and their brethren of more humble origin:

> One time there was a preacher that couldn't read, but he knowed most of the Book by heart, and preached better than lots of these here educated parsons. Sometimes he would tell funny stories about people in the Old Testament. Them stories ain't in the Bible at all, so maybe he just made 'em up as he went along.

. . . .

Some high-collared people in town thought it was wrong for a preacher to tell stories like that, but us home folks don't see no harm in it. We knowed that if God Almighty didn't like them sermons He could put a stop to it easy enough. And so long as the Lord God figured that our preacher was doing all right, who cares what them educated son-of-a-bitches think about it.[6]

Unhappiness with their economic condition also found its way into their musical idiom. The lyrics to a ballad entitled "Down on Penny's Farm" provided a tenant's view of life on a farm:

Come you Ladies and Gentlemen, listen to my song,
Sing it to you right, but you might think it's wrong.
May make you mad, but I mean no harm,
It's just about the renters on Penny's farm.
It's a hard times in the country out on Penny's farm.

. . . . .

You move out on Penny's farm,
Plant a little crop of 'bacco and a little crop of corn.
Come around to see you gonna slip and slid,
Till you get yourself a mortgage on everything you got.
It's a hard times in the country out on Penny's farm.

. . . . .

Hasn't George Penny got a flattering mouth,
Move you to the country in a little log house.
Got no windows but the cracks in the wall,
He'll work you all summer and rob you in the fall.
It's a hard times in the country out on Penny's farm.

. . . . .

You go in the fields you work all day,
Way into the night but you get no pay.
Promised some meat or a little bucket o' lard,
It's hard to be a renter on Penny's farm.
It's a hard times in the country out on Penny's farm.

. . . . .

Here George Penny he'll come into town.
With a wagonload of peaches not a one of them sound.
Got to have his money or somebody's check,

Pay him for a bushel and you don't get a peck.
It's a hard times in the country out on Penny's farm.

.   .   .   .   .

George Penny's renters they'll come into town.
With their hands in their pockets and their head ahanging down.
Go in the store and a merchant will say,
Your mortgage is due and I'm looking for my pay.
It's a hard times in the country out on Penny's farm.

.   .   .   .   .

Down in his pocket with a tremble in his hand.
Can't pay you all but I'll pay you what I can.
Then to the telephone the merchant make a call,
He'll put you on the chain gang if you don't pay it all.
It's a hard times in the country out on Penny's farm.

The song captured some of the bitterness of the tenant toward his land-lord. It also reflected the fear and uncertainty which characterized the system.

A Georgia textile mill song recalled the fact that women and chil-dren constituted most of the work force in many mills, and not all women were satisfied with their circumstances.

I worked in the cotton mill all my life,
I ain't got nothing but a barlow knife.
It's a hard times, cotton mill girls,
Hard times everywhere.

Chorus: It's a hard times, cotton mill girls,
A hard times, cotton mill girls,
Hard times, cotton mill girls,
Hard times everywhere.

In 1915 we heard it said,
"Move to cotton country and get ahead."
It's a hard times, cotton mill girls,
Hard times everywhere.

.   .   .   .   .

From Gilmer to Bartow is a long, long way,

Down Cartecay from Ellijay.
It's a hard times, cotton mill girls,
Hard times everywhere.

.   .   .   .   .

When I die don't bury me at all,
Just hang me up on the spinning room wall,
And pickle my bones in al-ki-hol.
It's a hard times, cotton mill girls.

The lyrics of poor white music can help reconstruct the past of indigent whites just as spiritual and work songs recapture the experience of the black poor. Hard times is a recurring theme and is less related to particular years than it is a pervasive commonplace. The year 1915, chronological focus of "Cotton Mill Girls," was a relatively good year for Southern farmers; but the promise of a better life in the mill village continued to lure women from the farms despite the "hard times," which actually awaited them.

During the decades following the Civil War poverty became institutionalized for Southern poor whites. They now produced products within the economic system, but this did not improve either their economic condition or their standing within the community. Those who remained on the land were plagued by one-crop agriculture, sagging cotton prices, and poor health, all of which hastened their slide into tenancy. Thousands sought a better life in coal camps and mill villages, but they improved their lot only marginally if at all.

One result of institutionalized poverty was a caste system in which the status of the white poor became to some degree fixed and rigid. Although the concept of caste system implies a lack of mobility which may exaggerate the crisis, the fact was that the plight of the bottom class worsened steadily during the final three decades of the nineteenth century. Divisions along class lines were obvious within communities, churches, and politics. Although such divisions were not expressed in classic Marxist terms of class consciousness, they did lead to visible efforts to organize and change policies that the poor blamed for their troubles. The Knights of Labor and the Populist party constituted two expressions of such unrest. Racism and irrational demagoguery were poor white attempts to find scapegoats for their unhappiness and were additional products of the wretchedness of their class.

If poor people failed to alter substantially the society that abused them, they were more successful at retaining from antebellum days a unique folk culture that helped them cope with their fate. Music and lore incorporated their experiences and helped them maintain dignity. Their medicinal remedies revealed an ingenuity and folk wisdom that is worth remembering; and their tales contained a lively wit that makes maudlin sympathy for them seem strangely misplaced.

Chapter Four

PROGRESS AND POVERTY
SOUTHERN STYLE
The 1920s and 1930s

Hard times affect people in different ways, but there is a certain common experience, a brotherhood of misery, which promotes sympathy. Suffering is so pervasive that it cannot be ignored or attributed entirely to personal failure of will. When a quarter of the American labor force was out of work in 1932, few citizens tried to explain the national disaster in terms of indolence. But when times are generally good, the poor become less visible and more easily dismissed. Society assumes that their indigence is a result of their own inadequacies, whether of body or spirit.

The two decades between 1920 and 1940 demonstrate both assumptions about the poor. The prosperity of the First World War years briefly opened avenues by which a few of the poor moved upward and obscured the millions who remained behind. The 1930s plunged the nation into so deep a crisis that everyone acknowledged the poor, and the federal government assigned the highest priority to reducing poverty.

Although the First World War was an international tragedy, the economic effect in the South brought a glimmer of hope. Military can-tonments and shipyards were located in the South to take advantage of the region's moderate climate, raw materials, and reserves of labor. Government purchases of Southern pine were so enormous that more than half the region's sawmills sold all their lumber to federal agencies, leaving none whatever for the public market. Wartime demands for Southern textiles set the industry on a course of expansion, which finally made it more productive than New England's mills in the 1930s. The demand for coal was so great that economic progress penetrated even the mountains of Appalachia. Harlan County, Kentucky, had only 169 coal miners in 1911; by 1923, it boasted 9,260. The years 1917–1919 were also the most prosperous in history for cotton farmers. The aver-age price per pound was twenty-seven cents during the war years, and in 1919 the price reached thirty-five cents a pound producing total reve-nue of over two billion dollars, the most valuable cotton crop in South-ern history.

Lillie Mae Flynt Beason lived on a forty-acre tenant farm near Wellington, Alabama, during the war. When their cotton sold for forty cents a pound, Homer Flynt, her father, bought his first mules. Owning mules meant that instead of surrendering half his crop, he kept two-thirds of his corn and three-fourths of his cotton. The family had its first outdoor toilet, and fifteen-year-old Lillie Mae made her first visit to the store. It was the spring of 1918, and her father promised that as soon as he borrowed money to plant his crop, he would take the teen-ager and her sister to the store and let them buy material for a dress. Fifty-eight years later she remembered the experience as if it had been yesterday:

> I bought a little pale blue linen—I don't know what she bought, but I know I made pleats. And you know linen is easy to pleat, but oh, how easy it is to wrinkle. I did the wrong thing, I found out later. Yet, that was the first buying that we did, actually go to a store and buy some-thing, and see bolts of cloth stacked on a shelf and a counter where they spread it out and measured it. That was all brand new to us. And we got shoes fitted for the first time. See, they'd just go buy shoes [usually], and they'd just buy them for whoever they thought they'd fit.[1]

Prosperity for the Flynts was a brief interlude. Homer Flynt remained a tenant farmer all his life; cotton prices fell after 1919 and the family moved again. Quickly conditions returned to pre-1917 levels until the 1930s when they got even worse.

That same pattern characterized the whole region. Paralyzing strikes in 1919–1920 demonstrated that not all Southern workers shared in the affluence of the ballyhoo years. As government expenditures declined following the Armistice, workers drifted back to mills and turpentine camps. Shipyards stood idle, their huge cranes and drydocks standing like silent skeletons. Workers who still had jobs were caught between skyrocketing inflation and job insecurity. They demanded wage increases that management refused, causing bloody strikes that spread from the phosphate mines of south Florida to the coal mines of Appalachia.

The Growth of Tenancy

The survival of poverty in the South during the prosperous 1920s is most easily observed in the agricultural system. By 1930, 55.5 percent of all Southern farms were operated by tenants. Since the percentage of Southerners engaged in agriculture was three times higher than in the rest of the country, agrarian poverty was far more significant a problem in the South.[2]

Other problems contributed to tenancy. The South's birth rate was significantly higher than any other region's, producing population growth at twice the national rate. Despite decades filled with arguments for diversified agriculture, King Cotton still reigned supreme. The cotton belt produced between eight and eighteen million bales, and the domestic market could absorb no more than six million. The rest had to be sold abroad, or it became a stifling surplus that held down the domestic price. During the early 1930s, production soared to fifteen million bales, and worldwide consumption sagged to twelve million, creating a huge surplus and driving the price down to 5.7 cents per pound in August 1932.

A special presidential committee studied the tenancy problem in

1937 and wrote a grim summary of conditions. In that year, two of every five American farmers were tenants, and two-thirds of all tenants and sharecroppers lived in the South. Sharecroppers who ranked lowest among tenants, comprised thirty-nine percent of the South's landless farmers. During the fifteen years from 1920 to 1935 white tenant families in the South increased by 300,000, while urban migration dropped the number of Negro tenant families by 70,000. Of the South's 1,831,000 tenant families in 1935, nearly two-thirds were white.

Even this grim landscape failed to measure the gravity of the crisis. Millions of Southerners who owned land stood on the precipice of tenancy because they farmed submarginal land, or plots too small to be efficient, or lived on eroded land. As late as 1945 the average farm in Alabama was only eighty-five acres, and, more significantly, fifty-four percent of the farms were under fifty acres; few farms of that size could afford modern equipment.

Mississippi provided one of the most distressing examples of the plight of rural poor whites. In 1930, 950,000 of the state's 2,100,000 people lived on tenant farms. Most families moved frequently looking for better treatment, houses, or land. Tenant houses usually were small frame buildings of two to four rooms, crudely constructed, unpainted, and lacking plumbing. Unscreened windows permitted mosquitoes to enter and contributed to a high incidence of malaria. Annual cash income was only seventy to eighty dollars per year and dropped as low as thirty-eight dollars in the lower Delta.

Mrs. Kathleen Knight was one of those 950,000 Mississippi tenant farmers during the early 1930s. Her mother, father, six brothers and sisters sharecropped a farm about seven miles from Cleveland, Mississippi. The landowner insisted that the family grow cotton, so they planted their garden of tomatoes, okra, and cucumbers between cotton rows. The water was bad and mosquitoes were so numerous that the family slept under nets. Malaria and typhoid were common among tenants, and pellagra ruined her father's health. The family received twenty dollars per month from March through August, a sum to be repaid when the cotton was gathered: "but, we were allowed to keep the [cotton] seed money to buy our food with up till we got our bills paid. . . . It was usually a rat race, I guess you would call it, because you just pay up and go back, and they would furnish you again."

Mrs. Knight also recalled social distinctions between landowners and tenants. The children of owners and tenants attended the same school: "but, now they got the . . . best deals in the school. Whenever the plays were put on, that's the only kind of recreation we had, . . . they were usually chose for the . . . best parts. . . . And of course we didn't think much about it. We was use to taking second place."

Tenancy took its toll on the alleged individualism and self-reliance of the poor white. He was economically and politically powerless, and like the black man, he learned to get along, to hold his tongue. White troublemakers were not so much in danger of losing their lives for an untoward gesture of defiance as were blacks; but they could be ordered off the land, and word of their temerity spread among the plantations. Mrs. Knight's father had one memorable clash with a plantation owner:

> Mrs. Knight: ". . . we had loaded up a bale of cotton on the wagon and he was going to carry it to the gin . . . And the landlord met him and told him to get down and go back to the field and keep picking. He told him 'no, he would take it.' And he went to climb up on the wagon to tell him to get down. And he [father] had a glass jug that we used to carry our water in, and he told him if he got up there he would knock him off with that jug; that he was taking that to town. Well, he let him carry it on, but I think that was the last time that he made an effort . . . to carry his own cotton. He just give in, I reckon."

> Interviewer: "Your daddy gave in?"

> Mrs. Knight: "Yea. It would affect you, you know, if you wanted to rent another plantation. Well, the way you did had a whole lot to do with where you could get it or not—a good rent. And they did a lot of moving around down there. I reckon they was just trying to find something better all [the] time—better house and better way of being treated."[3]

To Mrs. Knight, the Great Depression was not so much a cataclysm as just another event in a difficult life: "Well, we didn't know the difference in a depression, except . . . what we would hear. It just increased the fear a little bit of maybe not being able to get any food at all. We was just living on the bare necessities anyhow."

Mrs. Knight's oral memoir could be repeated by tens of thousands of white tenants. Writer James Agee spent several months during the summer of 1936 living with three white tenant families in Alabama. The Gudger and Woods families each contained six members and survived on ten dollars a month rations money provided them during the four months when cotton was growing. The Ricketts family of nine had to live on the same amount. Most half-sharing tenants received six dollars a bale for their share of the cottonseed. Gudger made three bales of cotton, each about five hundred pounds, and so could count on about eighteen dollars to live on during the picking and ginning, although he received nothing until his first bale was ginned. The most he ever made in a year was one hundred twenty-five dollars, and that came when the New Deal paid him to plow under his cotton. Most years he made twenty-five to thirty dollars, and one year in three he ended in debt.

Mill Workers

Not all the misery of the depression was on the farms; the textile industry also experienced hard times during the late 1920s, often with violent consequences. Many workers had come from tenant farms thinking that a better life awaited them in the mills. Although gainfully employed, they were still poor. In 1920 white men received wages of $1.75 to $2.50 a day, and white women from $1.34 to $1.84.

One of the most paternalistic textile facilities was Avondale Mills in Birmingham. Run by Donald Comer, Avondale experienced a common fate: progressively thinner profits in the 1920s and layoffs and strikes in the 1930s. The backgrounds of four Avondale workers were common industrywide. Alda Donahoo was the third of eight children born to a Tennessee tenant farmer. The family moved to Avondale in 1910 so that fourteen-year-old Alda and her father could work in the mill. Homer Butts began his textile career at a mill in Cordova, Alabama, at the age of eight. The son of a yeoman landowning farmer, he began work at Avondale in 1929. Syble Chandler was born into an Alabama tenant family and wanted to be a nurse; but her county had such limited funds for public education that she was able to complete only the seventh grade. She began working in the mill at age twenty. Willie Bell Neal's grandfather helped construct Avondale, and when she entered the mill in 1924, she represented the third generation of Neals to tend the spindles. As the eldest of seven children, she assumed responsibility for the entire family when her father died.[4]

Mill workers were often as transient as tenants, searching desperately for better conditions. In one mill, only two percent of the work force had been employed there for more than four years. One family of eight described their odyssey:

> We were married in Lake Mill. . . . We stayed there about a couple of years, then we farmed about a year. Then we went back to the cotton-mill and stayed about two or three years. Then we went to Woodburg and farmed for a year and a half. Then we went back to Lake Mill and worked about six months and then we moved to Smith County to this mill and stayed here about five years. In the spring we moved back to the Lake Mill and stopped there until Christmas. Then we took to farming for three or four months. We went back to the Hampton Mill and worked about two weeks and then moved to the Triffin Mill and stayed there two years. Then we moved back here and we have been here a year and a half. The last time we tried farming, the man who rented us the land quarreled over everything he furnished us. Then he didn't like our puppies and threatened to shoot them, so we moved.[5]

Paternalistic relations between bosses such as Donald Comer and laborers often dissolved under the pressure of declining markets, layoffs, and wage reductions. Wages fell to less than ten dollars a week in many mills during the late 1920s. Loray Mill in Gastonia, North Carolina, doubled work loads in 1929, discharged 1,300 employees, and reduced wages by twenty percent. Bitter strikes occurred in mills in Henderson, North Carolina (August, 1927), Elizabethton, Tennessee (March-May, 1929), Gastonia, North Carolina (April-September,

1929), and Marion, North Carolina (June-October, 1929). Many less violent but no less bitter strikes were called across the textile belt.

These strikes failed to win better conditions for workers from an industry hard hit by depression. Nor did labor gain even an organizational foothold in the textile industry. This failure has been attributed to many factors. Traditional Southern culture was too individualistic and too dominated by otherworldly religion. Southern workers were too mobile and apathetic. Communists and other radicals were involved in some Southern strikes, which provided a convenient target for conservatives to use against all organizing efforts. Also, Southern workers tended to organize only in response to a crisis; they did not view unions as a basis for continuous industrial relations.

Undoubtedly, Southern culture did inhibit the rise of unionism. Established Southern churches were largely apathetic about economic injustice and were often allied to the community's businessmen. Furthermore, the irreligious reputation of Communist organizers in places such as Gastonia alienated many religious mill hands.

Southern evangelicals, however, were not of one mind on unionism. A small minority of regularly ordained and lay ministers in Gastonia sympathized with the strikers. Representing sects that were otherworldly, they included no Methodists or Episcopalians. Two of them were Baptist ministers without regular churches to pastor who worked at the Loray Mill. Others were ministers of the Holiness church and the Church of God.

Although there was little overt support for the strikers from traditional elements of Southern culture, that culture supported them in different ways. Labor songs frequently borrowed the music of traditional hymns, and workers' notions of personal worth and justice were nourished by a religion that emphasized the inherent dignity of all God's creatures. Ella May Wiggins, twenty-nine-year-old mother of five and slain heroine of the Gastonia strikers, conveyed her most effective protests not in theoretical jargon but in powerful ballads, which had belonged to generations of Carolina poor whites. "We Shall Overcome," later adapted to the civil-rights movement, was a white hymn first utilized by Carolina poor whites in a CIO organizing drive. Although

A retired textile worker and carpenter L. A. House and his wife, Sylacauga, Alabama, around 1970. (*Everett Smith*)

Coal miners, near Birmingham, Alabama, early twentieth century. (*Birmingham Public Library*)

M. C. Sizemore, a retired coal miner, Stonega, Virginia, August 1974. (*Jerry W. Barrett*)

Young boys taking cotton to the gin in Alabama, around 1900. (*Carter D. Poland. Auburn University Archives*)

Southern folk culture was not a particularly congenial climate for labor protests, some elements of that culture sustained poor whites in their struggle for a decent life.

Southern laborers received less ambivalent support from the Democratic administration in Washington. The Fair Labor Standards Act, a keystone of New Deal labor policies, sought to raise substandard wages without substantially reducing employment. The minimum wages set by the FLSA had immediate impact on Southern industry. The government divided the textile industry into a number of categories. The average hourly earnings in two of these divisions in September 1939 were the second and fourth lowest paid in any industry listed in the survey conducted by the Bureau of Labor Statistics. When the FLSA applied a 32.5 cents minimum wage in July 1940, 55 percent of the workers in the men's clothing industry and 43 percent of those in the shirt industry were receiving less than this minimum. Thanks to federal minimum wage standards, salary differentials between Southern and Northern laborers in the same industries were reduced. The New Deal also sought to protect the rights of workers to organize collectively, although employers often found ways to circumvent federal regulations.

The Discovery of Southern Poor Whites

Americans became aware of Southern poverty when the conditions of poor whites became part of a national crisis. The nation always seems to be "discovering" some facet of the South, depending on what the nation's needs are at a particular moment. America in the 1920s needed a "benighted South," the New Deal "discovered" the poverty South, and in the 1960s America uncovered the "racist South." In truth, white poverty was ever present in the region and only intensified with the coming of the depression. Earlier generations of Americans—and Southerners—could have found it for the looking.

Southern poor whites usually attracted popular interest following some particular historical crisis. Popular literature about the South was concentrated in three periods. The first had occurred shortly after 1900 and corresponded to the Democratic party's attempt to enact whatever reforms were necessary to absorb the Populists. The second came in the 1930s when novelists and journalists dramatically portrayed the degradation of poor whites. This phase corresponded to a series of efforts to organize poor whites. The most recent discovery came in the 1960s as a result of concern for the rights of blacks and the poor.

During the depression, an array of gifted writers directed their talents toward the blighted South. Without their efforts to publicize the dimensions of white poverty, even less reform would have been possible. Throughout the early decades of the twentieth century, American intellectuals had been preoccupied with urban/industrial problems, and the tenant farmer had been ignored. It is small wonder, then, that the literature concerning poor whites before the 1930s was largely a regional literature. Furthermore, some novelists during the depression accepted older stereotypes about the poor, perpetuating and even expanding the image of shiftless, dull-witted degenerates. Erskine Caldwell, for instance, depicted his tenants as a comic, contemptible subspecie in novels such as *Tobacco Road, God's Little Acre,* and *Trouble in July.*

Even sympathetic literary treatment of the poor focused more on the person than on the economic system that produced him. Marjorie Kinnan Rawlings moved to the tiny north-central Florida community of Cross Creek in 1928. In her Pulitzer Prize-winning novel *The Yearling,* she captured the poignancy of a poor boy's coming of age in the Ocali, the big scrub country that later became the Ocala National Forest. Cecil Marie Matschat explored the life of the poor in *Suwanee River,* as did Dubose Heyward in *Angel,* Thomas Wolfe in *Look Homeward, Angel,* E. M. Roberts in *The Time of Man,* and Caroline Miller in *Lamb in His Bosom.*

No one is so famous for his portrayal of poor whites as William Faulkner. The Mississippi writer, more than any other novelist of the decade, depicted the poor white as something more than a primitive. In his novels published during these years, *Light in August* and *Sanc-*

tuary, he probed beneath the comic, provincial stereotype characteristic of Caldwell's tenants, to examine the individual consciousness of poor whites.

The work of James Agee also balanced the fiction of Caldwell. A Tennessean by birth, Agee had attended Exeter and Harvard before taking a job as a writer for *Fortune* magazine. He found the sophistication and secularism of New York City stifling, and accepted an offer from *Fortune* in the summer on 1936 to travel to east-central Alabama and live with white tenant families in preparation for an article.

Agee was fascinated with the possibilities of photography. It was the era of the camera, and pictures of tenants had appeared regularly in glossy magazines such as *Life* and *Look*. To assist Agee, the magazine employed photographer Walker Evans whose work for the Farm Security Administration contributed significantly to the entirely new genre of documentary photography. Agee and Evans spent July and August 1936 living with three white tenant families in Alabama—the Ricketts, Gudgers, and Woods—and recording visually and verbally impressions of tenant life.

It was a shattering emotional experience for both men, but especially for the sensitive Agee. *Fortune* decided not to publish the article, but Agee expanded the manuscript into a book entitled *Let Us Now Praise Famous Men,* which was published by Houghton Mifflin in 1941. It sold fewer than six hundred copies and reviewers either ignored or panned it. Despite the lack of critical acclaim, it was one of the most searing portrayals of white tenant life.

Innovative in makeup as well as in style, the book opened with thirty-one photographs without caption or explanation. The vacant gaze of tenant children challenged the American myth of the joys of rural childhood. Faces of tenant women were decades older than their age. Drab houses and despairing men blended into one disquieting reality. But the pages that followed did not give way to a mood of unrelieved despondency. Agee captured the strength and beauty of tenant lives. The dogtrot house lacking the slightest embellishment ("as if a hard thin hide of wood has been stretched to its utmost to cover exactly once, or a little less than once"), became an aesthetic mirror to an entire culture:

> It is put together out of the cheapest available pine lumber, and the least of this is used which will stretch a skin of one thickness alone against the earth and air; and this is all done according to one of the three or four simplest, stingiest, and thus most classical plans contrivable, which are all traditional to that country: and the work is done by half-skilled, half-paid men under no need to do well, who therefore take such vengeance of the world as they may in a cynical and part willful apathy; and this is symmetry and simpleness. Enough lines, enough off-true, that this symmetry is strongly yet most subtly sprained against its centers, into something more powerful than either full symmetry or deliberate breaking and balancing of "monotonies" can hope to be. A look of being earnestly hand-made, as a child's drawing, a thing created out of need, love, patience, and strained skill in the innocence of a race. Nowhere one ounce or inch spent with ornament, not one trace of relief or disguise: a matchless monotony, and in it a matchless variety: and this again throughout restrained, held rigid: and of all this, nothing which is not intrinsic between the materials of structure, the earth, and the open heaven.[6]

Agee's eye for detail riveted upon the degradation, which he described with equal skill. In some ways the book was a fusion of writer and subject; "Southern boy made good" came home from sophisticated colleges and the urbane secularism of New York City and rediscovered his own people in the clay hills of east-central Alabama. The explanation was a compelling one, for Agee's own sense of guilt, his disgust with himself and with the middle-class readers he anticipated, repeatedly broke through. His reaction to the condescension of most Americans toward tenants caused him to canonize them. He ignored the racism of poor whites as completely as he did their politics. Economic and political reforms were useless, and the context of his story was cosmic. His three families were damned from the start, and the task he set for himself was the depiction of their courage, their uniqueness, and the simple pleasures by which they sought to compensate for their fate.

Other studies were more dispassionate. Arthur F. Raper's book, *Preface to Peasantry,* written in 1936, centered on Greene and Macon counties, Georgia, where more than half the white farmers were tenants in 1930. In 1935 the University of North Carolina published *The Collapse of Cotton Tenancy* by Will Alexander, Charles S. Johnson, and Edwin D. Embree, a factual and moderate volume based on extensive field reports of rural conditions, and still recognized as one of the best brief economic and sociological surveys of tenancy in the 1930s. Skillful publicity for the book by Johnson, Embree, and Alexander popularized the tenancy crisis nationwide and even elicited an affirmative critique from President Franklin D. Roosevelt, who called it the best book yet written on Southern agriculture.

The New Deal

Such works attracted a national audience, but Southern politicians demonstrated little interest. Poor whites played a minor role in the depression-era politics of the region. Plagued historically by apathy, lack of education, and rural isolation, they faced the more specific hurdle of the poll tax. The tax was cumulative if unpaid each year, and a tax of six or eight dollars made voting impossible for tenant farmers. Also, politics was dominated by "courthouse gangs" of affluent planters, merchants, and industrialists, who took little interest in the plight of their poorer neighbors.

The few economic liberals who managed to win elections with the backing of textile workers, coal miners, and other laborers entered state legislatures that were malapportioned and unresponsive. Even had state governments possessed the will to act, they had few financial resources during the 1930s. Such economic liberals as were elected to Congress provided support for New Deal measures which did most to relieve the distress of poor Southern whites.

Federal attempts to assist Southern tenants ran into immediate difficulties. The New Deal focus on unemployment was partly responsible. Although unemployment was a serious regional problem, the Southeastern rate was below the national average. The South's larger

crises were low productivity and wages. The one exception to this economic generalization was farm unemployment. The eleven Southeastern
states (omitting Texas but including Kentucky) had a higher rate of
agricultural unemployment by 1937 than the nation as a whole. This
situation was largely the result of rural youth who could not find jobs
and the displacement of tenant farmers.

A cornerstone in Roosevelt's program to help farmers was the
Agricultural Adjustment Act of May 1933. It attempted to reduce
acreage devoted to cotton by paying farmers to divert land to other
crops. In the five-year period from 1934 to 1939, eleven million acres
were taken out of cotton production. In the period 1938–1942, government programs permitted only twenty-seven million acres of cotton
to be planted, and farmers actually planted three million acres less than
the maximum allowable. Although this policy promoted agricultural
diversification, it was less successful in its primary objective. Farmers
removed marginal lands from production, fertilized remaining soil
heavily, and produced almost as much cotton as before.

The act seriously injured tenant farmers. In 1933 some landlords
plowed up their share of the crops, receiving government subsidies,
while their tenants were denied such aid. Others signed acreage agreements with the Department of Agriculture without any mention of tenants whatever. Landowners dominated the local committees, which
administered the acreage reduction programs, and they also dominated
the Cotton Section of the AAA, which negotiated contracts. Acreage
contracts negotiated in 1934 and 1935 established ceilings for sharecroppers of eleven percent of the subsidy payments and limited tenants
to fifteen percent. By 1934 such inequities attracted national attention.
Socialist Norman Thomas toured the Arkansas Delta and announced
that AAA policy was driving thousands of tenants into the status of
farm laborers or off the land entirely. Although the extent of tenant
displacement cannot be determined, it occurred in many locations.

Ironically, the first New Deal program to substantially improve
conditions among poor farmers grew out of New Deal relief plans, not
out of the Agriculture Department. The Federal Emergency Relief
Administration, headed by Harry Hopkins, stirred controversy from its

inception. When the agency established its Rural Rehabilitation program in 1934, the FERA staff divided between agriculturists who proposed that rehabilitation credit should be made available only on the basis of sound banking principles, and social workers who viewed the program as an experiment in improving the general life of the poor. The social worker contingent wanted to encourage self-direction among the poor and minimize supervision over funds. Landowners and conservative politicians condemned the program because relief payments were sometimes more than sharecroppers normally made.

Implementation of the relief program posed additional problems. The Division of Rural Rehabilitation provided grants and loans for seed, fertilizer, livestock, and farm tools to enable farmers to keep off relief rolls. Liberal administrators within the division complained that these policies dealt only with the temporary effect of the depression and not with chronic rural poverty. One state relief director reported from Kentucky in November 1934, that "the average of rural classes on relief in Kentucky have never had an adequate standard of living. In the mountain counties . . . where from 30 to 60 per cent of the population is on relief, average standards of living are perhaps higher now than they have ever been—certainly no lower." A similar report from mountainous northwestern Arkansas noted that families rarely received more than twenty-five dollars a year in cash and existed on a diet of four or five items even in "normal times."[7]

The Rural Rehabilitation Division was typical of many New Deal agencies that ultimately promised more than they delivered. At its peak in April 1935, it reached only a fraction of the South's poor, and it bypassed the most impoverished altogether. For those it touched, the division brought improvement, especially by raising them from the bottom rung of tenancy, sharecropping, to a higher level. But it touched so few. In the Appalachian-Ozark region, 23.5 percent of the tenants participated in the program; in the Southeastern cotton belt, only 3.9 percent of the tenants received assistance.

The Rural Rehabilitation program lasted only from April 1934 until July 1935, when it was replaced by more permanent agencies. Its basic philosophy of combining credit and guidance was continued and refined by subsequent New Deal agencies. Also, from the published field reports of rehabilitation workers came the earliest proposals for government provision of land to the chronically rural poor. Alexander, Johnson, and Embree called for federal provision of land in their edited field reports published in 1935 under the title, *The Collapse of Cotton Tenancy*. There was much political disagreement over implementation of the idea, and not until the Southern Tenant Farmers' Union publicized the proportions of the economic crisis was the Farm Security Administration created. The major contribution of the Farm Security Administration was to add long-term programs to the emergency grants carried over from the earlier era. The catalyst for the formation of the FSA came from an unlikely source. Neither government experts nor social workers, but the vigorous exertion of the poor themselves brought their case before the nation.

Tenant farmers found a curious champion in H. L. Mitchell. His grandfather had been a Baptist preacher and small farmer in Alabama, and his family "came down the agricultural ladder" like so many others in the late nineteenth century. His family moved to Tennessee where his father found work in a sawmill. Like most farm children, Mitchell began chopping cotton about the time he began school. By 1920 he was a sharecropper when a calamitous drop in prices left him barely enough money to purchase a suit of clothes, his only reward for a year's labor. During the early twenties he married and moved to the Arkansas Delta; but tenant conditions were so bad that he went into town to work. He ran a cleaning business in Tyronza, Arkansas, while peddling Socialist doctrine that he read in the works of Upton Sinclair.

When the depression hit, New Deal policies administered through the Department of Agriculture only seemed to worsen the crisis among Mitchell's tenant neighbors, and some townspeople suffered almost as badly. He witnessed a near-riot in Truman, Arkansas, where some workers laid off by the Singer Sewing Machine Company, having gone several days without food, threatened to break into local food stores to take what they needed. In July 1934, Mitchell, with J. R. Butler, E. B. McKinney, and other friends, organized the Southern Tenant Farmers' Union. The union attracted both former Klansmen and Negro croppers in a coalition born of desperation. Mitchell, who also served as state secretary of the Arkansas Socialist party, influenced the S.T.F.U. declaration of principle that spoke of two agricultural classes: "actual tillers of the soil who have been ground down to dire poverty," and their landlords and exploiters. Although not all white members overcame their hostility to blacks, the S.T.F.U. became a biracial, militantly class-conscious tenant union. Union meetings frequently were held in rural churches and many S.T.F.U. leaders were ministers, black and white. Members sang traditional church melodies substituting militant new class lyrics. Local landowners, aided by state officials, tried to destroy the union by evicting sharecroppers and by occasional violence, but the resulting national publicity directed on the remote hamlet of Tyronza had a different effect.

Socialist leader Norman Thomas visited the town in February 1934, and told the nation that never in America had he seen such abject poverty. Mitchell and J. R. Butler followed Thomas's statement with a writing campaign criticizing New Deal policies and blasting the alliance between Department of Agriculture officials and local landlords. Shrewdly relying upon agitation and publicity rather than ineffectual strikes by its 31,000 members, the S.T.F.U. became one of the South's most important organized protest movements. It precipitated a division within the staff of the Agriculture Department and, by calling attention to violence aimed at S.T.F.U. members, persuaded Congress to establish the LaFollette Civil Liberties Committee, which launched an extensive investigation of violations of the civil liberties of tenants. But the S.T.F.U.'s most lasting significance was its function as a left-of-center critic of New Deal agricultural policies. The nationwide attention it received proved a major factor in President Roosevelt's decision following his reelection in 1936 to appoint the President's Committee on Farm Tenancy; this committee, in turn, laid the groundwork for the Bankhead-Jones Farm Tenancy Act of 1937.

The membership of the President's Committee ranged from W. L. Blackstone representing the S.T.F.U. to Edward A. O'Neal of the conservative Farm Bureau Federation. Many members, such as Will Alexander and Dr. Charles Johnson of Fisk University, had already demonstrated their concern for tenants. They made an honest effort to wrestle with the complexities of agricultural economics, and their research provided a factual base for reform. Although the major focus of the investigation was on the bottom rung of the agricultural ladder—sharecroppers and farm laborers—the committee also dealt with farmers who owned as little as one-fifth of the land they farmed, and with proprietors who worked submarginal land or farms too small to provide anything more than mere survival. Mobility among farmers over the previous few years had been down, with low status becoming ever more rigid, "forcing imprisonment in a fixed social status from which it is increasingly difficult to escape."

Committee members noted that the most critical problems of tenancy were in the South, a theory that influenced their ameliorative proposals. Facing the broad question of tenant life, they conceded realistically that providing easy credit in order to convert tenants into landowners would not eliminate "ignorance, poverty, malnutrition, morbidity, and social discrimination by which many farm tenant families are handicapped." They proposed that the Resettlement Administration serve as the nucleus of a new Farm Security Administration to deal with the primary concern of the committee: providing economic security for farmers. The administration should purchase land that would be leased to tenants for a probationary period. When tenants demonstrated sufficient management skills, they would be allowed to purchase the land. Borrowing from the experiences with rural rehabilitation, they proposed loans to provide machinery, livestock, feed, seed, and fertilizer, along with technical guidance. Submarginal land should be purchased by the government at slightly more than four dollars per acre and developed for recreational use. The committee also proposed state action to supervise contracts between tenants and owners in order to protect the civil liberties of tenants. Reflecting the influence of S.T.F.U. publicity, the members noted that tenants seeking to bargain collectively had been denied constitutional rights and subjected to physical violence.

Dissenting reports were filed by both extremes on the committee. Blackstone of S.T.F.U. protested the majority recommendation that the Farm Security Administration be placed under the Department of Agriculture, an agency which he claimed had aided only the upper one-third of American farmers. The ideal system of farm security was not the small homestead envisioned by the majority report; he argued for farmers' cooperatives under federal supervision and proposed an even stronger statement on civil liberties as well as committee endorsement of the unionization of farm workers. Edward O'Neal of the Farm Bureau Federation filed a dissenting report opposing creation of the Farm Security Administration and all other federal meddling in the tenant system.

The committee recommendations were presented to Congress in 1937 in the form of the Bankhead-Jones Farm Tenancy bill. Determined opposition from conservatives emasculated the bill. The Farm Security Administration was established, but the agency could not sell land to tenants. Roosevelt still believed that liberal administration of the agency could save most of the original objectives, and he appointed the former Nashville Methodist minister Will Alexander to head the agency. Alexander selected like-minded Southern liberals to assist him, and the entire agency was dominated by Southern reformers. By the end of 1941, the Farm Security Administration had provided loans to 20,748 tenants for the purchase of land; but during the same period, lack of funds required the agency to deny twenty applications for every one it granted. In Arkansas, where the entire fracas began, out of a total of 151,759 tenant families, only 1,399 received loans. Conservatives resented even the modest concessions won by tenants and eliminated the Farm Security Administration in 1944, replacing it with the weaker Farmers Home Administration.

At the end of the depression, the tenant problem still was unresolved. Even the most liberal New Deal agencies, such as the Farm Security Administration, were so sensitive to charges of communism and socialism and so susceptible to conservative congressional sniping that they fell far short of solving the complex problems of poor whites in the South. At the same time, left-of-center critics of Roosevelt largely ignored that he at least publicized the plight of the South's poor, and that the FSA staff made herculean efforts, which dramatically altered the lives of tens of thousands of tenant families. The failure of the FSA to eliminate the problem of tenancy should not obscure its efforts.

Carl Forrester, a peanut farmer who lived in Houston County, Alabama, was a typical recipient of the benefits of the FSA. Born in 1906, married in 1928, he began sharecropping in 1927 and continued until 1941. Carl Forrester's loan was one of those approved by FSA in the fall of 1941. The agency:

bought us this place here [100 acres] . . . and helped us get started, back us up, furnished us and all. And, we worked here two years with mules. And in the fall of '44, Mr. Borland—[he] was the supervisor—[By 1944 the FSA had become the Farmers' Home Administration] give me permission to sell them old mules and plow stocks and two horse wagon and cultivator—walkin' cultivators what I had then—and buy a used one row tractor. A little ole A Farmall. And we started . . . the first crop in '44 with a tractor.[8]

The FSA/FHA administrators provided technical advice on crops, livestock, and markets. Forrester used a relative's service pay during World War II to purchase forty more acres. His credit then firm, he borrowed money from a bank to finance the purchase of one hundred twenty additional acres. A good farmer and hard worker, he abandoned cotton for wheat, then turned to hog raising, and finally converted to peanuts, corn, and soy beans. By 1970 he was a proud and prosperous man who had set his son up in farming. Carl Forrester did not consider the FSA/FHA a conservative failure; but Forrester represented a small fraction of the South's poor whites.

The farm tenancy report was only the first salvo in a double-barreled assault by the New Deal on Southern poverty. The following year, 1938, the President's National Emergency Council issued its report. Clark Forman, head of the Power Division of the Public Works Administration, supervised the report, which was prepared in less than a month. It emphasized the unfulfilled needs of the South and, inferentially, suggested a political purge of Southern Democratic conservatives who had aligned with Republicans to weaken such progressive legislation as Bankhead-Jones. The sixty-four page document detailed the unfulfilled agenda in the country's "economic problem, no. 1." The report predictably infuriated conservatives, and Roosevelt's attempt to purge them in the 1938 off-year elections failed.

Southern Poverty and Southern Intellectuals

In the long run, no single group did more to provide strategies for ending Southern poverty than Southern intellectuals. Just as Southern novelists had played a central role in publicizing poor whites, the region's intellectuals outlined her options. For two decades the South had squirmed beneath a fusillade of charges ranging from sophisticated attacks on folk religion to tactless references to an economic miracle that could be wrought if every Southerner wore shoes. Within the South bright young men and women, torn between their love for the South's regional culture and their anger at its economic plight, debated what ought to be done. Their responses to criticism and poverty varied. The first reaction belonged to the "it's not so" or "you're one too" school of Southern thought, which either denied the criticism or charged that regional conditions elsewhere were no better. All Southerners and even their mules wore shoes, they argued. All too often "it" was so, and the problems diminished none at all with the discovery that Northerners suffered from similar maladies. A small school of journalists and reformers confronted the region's problems and courageously suggested political and economic solutions. But a more influential approach came from a band of Vanderbilt University intellectuals who defended agrarianism and wrote a trenchant critique of industrial society.

A group of poets at Vanderbilt, revolting against attacks on the South during the 1920s, realized that economic progress would inevitably, and in their view negatively, influence Southern folkways. They were among the earliest Southerners to realize that Southern poverty had produced a culture of great value, which might be jeopardized by "progress." Recruiting several faculty colleagues among social scientists, they published their classic tract *I'll Take My Stand* in 1930. Although the academicians obviously felt more affection for farm life than many tenant farmers did, their critique was important. They argued intellectually what many tenants felt intuitively: that life on the land was not all bad despite the poverty. (One need only read James Agee's *Let Us Now Praise Famous Men* to understand how strongly the land bound the poor, how agonizing was their decision to leave it even for that illusive prosperity that so often was promised and so seldom realized.)

The Agrarians idealized the Jeffersonian society of subsistence farmers. Urban business and professional classes should occupy a secondary economic, social, and political role to the farmer. The inconvenience and poverty of rural life seemed trivial when compared with the urban malaise of the city. But the Agrarians were intellectuals, and their movement did not reach the masses. Furthermore, many Southern intellectuals rejected the Agrarian notion that the best life for the region's common folk was subsistence agriculture. The Agrarians overglamorized the antebellum South. They also lacked the coherent vision and program necessary to make subsistence agriculture attractive to the poor.

The Agrarians believed that a majority of people must own productive property if society was to remain free and prosperous, and the preponderance of tenants among Southern farmers troubled them. Historian Herman Clarence Nixon, who authored the essay "Whither Southern Economy" in *I'll Take My Stand,* proposed agricultural diversification; but his utopian world of subsistence farmers banished class consciousness. In fact, one of his chief criticisms of industrialism was the prospect of "an inter-class struggle that may usher in a socialistic receivership. . . ." Nine years of depression substantially modified his stand. Together with Dr. Charles Johnson of Fisk University, Rupert Vance, a sociology professor at the University of North Carolina, and social critic Arthur Raper, Nixon served on the Southern Policy Association's tenancy subcommittee. This group strongly recommended S.T.F.U. style cooperatives to the President's Committee on Tenancy. Nixon's book *Forty Acres and Steel Mules,* published by the University of North Carolina Press in 1939, showed his transition most completely. The volume effectively employed 148 Farm Security Administration photographs by Walker Evans and others to depict the grim life of tenant farmers and laborers. Nixon's book appeared in an era when class conflict served increasingly as a basis for interpreting the South's past, and it sparked a lively debate. A young historian, C. Vann Woodward, whose class-oriented biography of Populist leader Tom Watson had appeared in 1938, reviewed Nixon's work. Woodward editorialized that the exploitation of the South had been twofold: the nation had abused the region, and some Southerners had exploited other Southerners. His review was a strong class argument in favor of approaching the South through the experiences of common folk, tenants, and laborers of both races. He was pleased that Nixon had moved closer to a class analysis since his essay in *I'll Take My Stand*.

One of the coauthors of the 1930 treatise immediately joined debate with Woodward. Poet Donald Davidson chided the historian for spending so much time studying the Populists that he had lost perspective. Pointing to the failure of the Populists to win political power, Davidson argued that the South was too agrarian to suit a Marxist approach to history. Jeffersonian agrarianism and sectional conflict furnished a more reliable guide to the South's past. Davidson added that the class approach obliterated the color line, thus confusing a solution to the racial problem that could be obtained only by keeping the Negro in a separate category.

The debate among Southern intellectuals that began with the Agrarians entered a new phase in 1941 with the publication of Wilbur J. Cash's brilliant, tortured volume *The Mind of the South*. Focusing on the darker episodes in the region's past, Cash probed the Southerner's propensity for violence, intolerance, suspicion of new ideas, exaggerated individualism, attachment to myth, false values, and excessive emotionalism. Cash divided the population into three classes—rich, poor, and black—then explained how the rich, though less numerous, had managed to remain in control by feeding the poor white a pabulum of plantation romance and racial mythology.

The initial response to the essay brought applause for its frankness, realism, and its emphasis on race and class. Donald Davidson dissented again, questioning Cash's three-class dichotomy, and the passing years modified the initial estimate of the work. Cash overemphasized the degree of white racial solidarity, and his book was more a discussion of some aspects of the Southern temper than a compelling analysis of the Southern mind. He notably omitted the Populist period and organized labor, perhaps because they did not fit his thesis.

The most enduring contribution to the intellectual debate over Southern white poverty came from Professor Howard Odum and programs at the University of North Carolina. A Georgian by birth, Odum graduated from Emory University and in 1920 became head of the Department of Sociology and director of the School of Public Welfare at Chapel Hill. He brought with him a background in the study of Negro life and folk society, which he broadened to include poor whites. Through his summer institutes, graduate students, his own research and publications, and a new journal, *Social Forces,* he began to define a unique regional mystique, with identifiable origins, problems, and resources.

Odum's work focused on folk culture, to which poor whites had made important contributions. These unique folkways had produced a distinctive society, and, although he favored federal help to solve regional problems, he insisted that such programs must recognize regional distinctions. This regionalist philosophy insisted that any programs to resolve Southern ills must recognize the unique individualism produced by prolonged contact with nature. They must acknowledge that national culture was not blandly homogenous, but richly variegated and firmly bound to place. Despite Odum's advocacy of federal help and planning, which made regionalism anathema to some conservatives, it stood counter to the cosmopolitan urbanism and economic determinism of the times. Regionalism called for a sensitive new appraisal of a poor white culture that was misunderstood and negatively stereotyped. It warned that the mere distribution of resources and technology without regard to folk life would not solve the South's problems. Unfortunately, later generations forgot Odum's wisdom, economics replaced folk sociology as a frame of reference, and government planners proposed to solve the South's woes by constructing interstate highways or by similar economic programs.

Some of Odum's students, Mildred Rutherford Mell in particular, studied Southern poor whites and collected much statistical data on which to base New Deal programs. Rupert Vance, Odum's colleague in the sociology department at Chapel Hill, also helped popularize the concept of farmer cooperatives as a member of the tenancy committee of the Southern Policy Association.

Odum's focus on folkways contributed to a revival of interest in the South's common people. Interest in folk culture tended to follow a pattern. Often it began as the result of a negative stimulus such as outside criticism. Then a few intellectuals both inside and outside the region became conscious of the uniqueness of cultural heritage. A revival of interest in the traditional culture followed which frequently brought political change. Whatever the pattern, Southern poor white culture began to captivate a widening audience. Representatives of the Russell Sage Foundation led by John Campbell and his wife Olive had already produced pioneering studies of Appalachian music and crafts in the 1920s. Then in 1935 the *Tennessee Folklore Society Bulletin* began. Two years later the *Southern Folklore Quarterly* was launched. Although these publications were part of the regionalist revival sparked by Odum, their focus was more broadly humanistic.

Religion and the Poor

As part of their general concern for poor white culture, some Southern intellectuals cautiously began to study folk religion. The fundamentalist strife of the 1920s was too recent to allow intellectuals to seriously weigh the possibility that evangelical religion might serve a positive function for the poor, but some conceded that there were subtle class differences within Christianity. Intellectuals had argued for decades that culture played an important if not dominant role in religion; but they had not pursued their argument to its conclusion. If a conservative cultural milieu caused Christianity to defend the economic and social status quo, a class-conscious culture influenced religion in the opposite direction. Poor whites who became increasingly aware of their poverty could either dismiss the church as essentially escapist and conservative, as H. L. Mitchell did, or they could identify with sects whose emotionalism or nonconformist theology set them apart from the more conservative church types. Liston Pope's classic study of Gastonia, North Carolina, mill workers, *Millhands and Preachers,* concluded that ministers of the Pentecostal and Baptist sects who stood outside the dominant economic and religious life of the community were the only preachers who sided with strikers. H. L. Mitchell noticed the same phenomenon, agreeing that many Arkansas leaders of the Southern Tenant Farmers' Union were ministers, blacks and whites, of Baptist or Holiness sects.[9]

Churches reflected Southern white poverty as thoroughly as other institutions. A 1923 survey of rural churches in seventy Southern counties found that tenant farmers were less frequently members of churches than landowners. Church membership declined as white farm tenancy increased. In many Appalachian mountain counties, the church membership was less than one-eighth of the population. Most rural churches did not hold services every Sunday, and only twenty percent had full-time pastors. Seven out of ten of the ministers had no college or seminary training, and forty-eight percent of them were bivocational, depending on farming, teaching, mill work, or business for part of their income. No other region had such a high percentage of ministers dependent on an outside job. One-seventh of them earned less than five hundred dollars per year. In some ways, this Southern ministerial phenomenon made Southern rural preachers more able to identify with their congregations, because many of them, especially Baptists and Pentecostals, were as poor as the people they served. It also explains why ministers occasionally became union organizers since many of them were also tenants, miners, or mill workers.

The fact that tenants did not attend church so regularly as owners did not mean that they took religion less seriously. Rural Christianity provided a sense of purpose for otherwise dismal lives. Tenants noted that in time of trouble, they found a resource: "If He had not stood by me, I would not have lived through the trouble I have had." Asked what difference it would make in their lives if they became convinced that no loving God cared for them, one replied: "I'd feel like I was lost." Another responded: "Wouldn't have any encouragement then sure enough. Would just end it up sometime."

The perceptions of Odum and Vance that solutions to poverty had to take into account the unique folk culture provided a firm base for future federal programs. Unfortunately, the national mood changed rapidly as war clouds gathered over Europe and reform ceased to be a national priority.

The depression that brought widespread suffering to many Americans had less damaging significance to Southern poor whites. The poverty that had plagued them for years worsened, but at last America recognized their existence and their problems. Through both their own efforts and the attention of Southern intellectuals, their plight became well known, and the New Deal devised programs that, for all their limitations, made some progress toward solving individual troubles even if they could not eliminate white poverty in the South.

A few poor whites became disillusioned and joined Communist labor unions or the Socialist Southern Tenant Farmers' Union. Desperate economic conditions made strange political coalitions, and men who had been Klansmen in the 1920s joined integrated unions. But most poor whites accepted their condition fatalistically and found solace in their religion and folkways. Most of them not only endured the wretchedness of the depression; they even maintained their dignity and self-respect.

CHAPTER FIVE

SOUTHERN POVERTY FORGOTTEN AND DISCOVERED—AGAIN

On April 17, 1964, Selz C. Mayo, chairman of the sociology department at North Carolina State University and a former student of Howard Odum, made a shocking pronouncement to the Southern Sociological Society: "The South that you and I knew—at least, the one that many of us knew personally—just three or four decades ago is no more." Brandishing data on socioeconomic change since the depression, he made a good case for his provocative introduction. Sharecropping and cotton production had declined simultaneously; the South had made significant strides in redistribution of income, health, and education, had narrowed income differentials with other regions, had diversified its agriculture and industrialized its economy. He believed that new attitudes among Southerners had preserved the best of Southern culture while eliminating divisive sectionalism.

When examined superficially, the changes to which Mayo alluded seemed to have transformed the South; upon more careful investigation, the predicament of poor whites was not so different after all. Economic definitions of poverty became dominant, and solutions were focused more narrowly. Projects sponsored by federal, regional, and state agencies entangled the poor in a web of bureaucracy and complex legislation. Despite much progress wrought by sincere, oftentimes idealistic, people, the poor remained in staggering numbers. For nearly a quarter century following 1940, America forgot Southern poverty, only to rediscover it in the mid-1960s.

Obscuring the Poor

When poverty was perceived as essentially an economic condition, it became a quantifiable problem, susceptible to graphs, charts, and statistics. Even culture was evaluated as a primary factor producing indigence; it was part of the problem to be treated along with its statistical symptoms. When programs, private or public, produced economic growth lines on statistical tables, this progress meant that the poor were being absorbed, their debilitating culture giving way before the more salutary mainstream.

The South's excellent climate and labor surplus attracted both federal and private investment during the early 1940s. The government spent an estimated four billion dollars, more than a third of its total expenditures on military facilities, in the South. War-related industry expended four-and-one-half billion dollars more during the same period. Towns grew into cities, and thousands of poor people were absorbed into the lower middle class.

Federal regional development further transformed the South. The Tennessee Valley experienced a substantial increase in nonagricultural employment and a decline in farm jobs during the 1940s. Judged by virtually any economic indicator, the lives of the 3,225,000 people in the Tennessee Valley were improving at a rate substantially faster than the rest of the country.

Other state and regional projects helped close the economic gap between the South and the nation. Creation of the National Planning Association's Committee on the South in 1947 was symbolic of economic dominance in Southern regional development. State development boards provided long-range planning, and in 1965 Congress added the Appalachian Regional Planning Commission.

Economists believed that many of the remaining obstacles to industrialization were cultural, not economic. One leading economist, William H. Nicholls, saw the basic issue facing the South after 1930 as the Old South with its agrarian-aristocratic tradition, represented by the Vanderbilt group, versus the New South advocates of Northern style industrial society. Nicholls included in the latter category every-one from Henry Grady to Howard Odum, Rupert Vance, and W. J. Cash. The New South had made progress only at the expense of the old, and it could triumph only if "many of those still-strong qualities of mind and spirit which have made the South distinctive largely disap-pear." He believed that the agrarian order with its rigid social structure, undemocratic politics, lack of social responsibility, and conformity of thought and behavior must give way to industrialism.

The changes in the South's economy following the depression could be divided into five categories: labor surplus and out-migration, tech-nological change, the expansion and diversification of industry, agri-cultural diversification, and urbanization. The government contributed meaningfully to the discussion with two major publications. In Octo-ber 1946, the *Monthly Labor Review* published by the U. S. Bureau of Labor devoted a special issue to labor and economic change in the South. The March 1968 issue returned to the same topic with even bet-ter results. Adopting a uniform definition of the South as the eleven former Confederate states plus Kentucky and Oklahoma, the articles probed an area of 843,812 square miles.

This region boasted the highest birth rates in America, creating a constant source of cheap labor. Such fecundity, in turn, produced three closely related phenomena. Usually the South experienced a steady out-migration of labor, which kept its population growth within man-ageable limits; some two-and-a-half million people, mostly poor, left for the North and the West during the 1940s. Secondly, surplus labor moved from the rural South into towns and cities. Finally, the region remained attractive to low-wage, labor-intensive industries such as textile mills, lumber and wood products, and furniture.

Cheap, unskilled, unorganized labor had long been one of the South's best advertised commodities. During the greatest period of Southern manufacturing growth between 1947 and 1958, employment increased most rapidly in the lowest-wage category, and the region received less than its share of more desirable high-wage jobs.

Despite the preponderance of low-wage industry, significant increases in almost every category of employment and manufacturing caused even cautious Southerners in the 1950s to proclaim that the long-heralded New South had finally arrived. Average wages rose faster than the national average. Per capita income increased at a rate one-third greater than in the rest of the U. S. in the 1940s, and one-fifth faster in the 1950s. Despite such improvements, most Southern economic indices still ranked well below the national average.

The Tenacity of White Poverty

Beneath the prosperous surface of the 1940s and 1950s, poor whites remained in large numbers. They could be subdivided geographically into Appalachian poor whites, those who lived in the rural, cotton-producing Core South, and industrial workers living in the urban South. They were also subject to differing definitions of poverty. Since 1940 poverty has been defined in three ways: the Social Security Administration has maintained that poverty means insufficient income to acquire the calories necessary for physical health; the Census Bureau defines it as a minimum family income established at varying amounts for different-sized families; and sociologists contend that it is a folk culture that isolates the poor because of their different values and attitudes.

Regardless of how poverty was defined, poor whites suffered most from agricultural changes: declining cotton markets, rising agricultural production costs that required mechanization in order to reduce labor expense, out-migration of rural labor, and a variety of technological innovations, especially cheap tractors. As foreign markets were lost, American cotton farmers were forced to sell on a domestic market at the same time that competition from paper and synthetic fibers increased. By 1945 no solid cotton belt was left in the South.

Mechanization and Dislocation of the Poor

This decline brought mechanization and diversification to the old cotton belt. Farmers with large holdings replaced work animals and tenants with tractors and cotton pickers. Pike County, for instance, had been one of the three leading cotton-producing counties in Alabama for most of the early twentieth century; mechanization, however, displaced thousands of poor Pike County farmers, and the number of mules and horses, symbols of marginal, subsistence farming, declined from a peak of 6,623 in 1920 to only 29 in 1964. In 1930, seventy-five percent of all farmers in Pike County had been tenants compared to only thirty percent in 1964. Most of the tenants had not been absorbed into the landowning class. They had been forced off the land or out of the county.

Mechanization was practical only for large, profitable farms, so the pattern of technological change varied widely in Alabama. In the rich soil of the Tennessee Valley, between ten and twenty percent of the farms had tractors in 1945; but on Sand Mountain, a fertile plateau in northeast Alabama with a virtually all white rural farm population, only three to six percent owned tractors in that same year. Large, mechanized cotton farms produced a bale of cotton per acre, but seventy-five percent of all Southeastern farms produced less than eight bales of cotton and averaged only about six-tenths of a bale per acre.

The total number of people affected by dislocation was substantial. While farm families constituted only 7 percent of the total number of families in America in 1960, they included 16 percent of the poor. Of the more than sixteen million rural persons in poor families in 1960, three-fourths were white, and over half of these lived in the South, a figure of over 6,000,000.

Mechanization had its most profound effect within the Core South. In 1943 International Harvester's mechanical cotton picker made its appearance in the South's cotton belt. This machine reduced labor requirements from 160 manhours to produce a bale of cotton to 28 hours. The estimated job loss, mainly in the Core South, was 2,291,000 family workers. Economic growth in Southern industry absorbed a little more than one quarter of this displaced farm labor, but migration and deepening poverty awaited the rest.

Even within the Core South where most poverty was among blacks, there were pockets of white deprivation. In one small South Georgia town in 1949, 26.4 percent of the community's population fell into the bottom socioeconomic class. Although most of the poor were blacks, 10.4 percent of those in the lowest class were white.

Many Southern whites displaced after World War II joined a migration to northern cities. Although they were stereotyped as hillbillies, many of them came from the Coastal Plain. Eleven Southeastern states (including Kentucky but excluding Texas and Oklahoma) contained 1,005 counties in 1960, and 549 of them lost population during the decade of the 1950s. In Arkansas, 69 of 75 counties suffered a loss; 45 of 67 Alabama counties experienced a net drop, as did 87 of Kentucky's 120 counties. Even at the state level the South lagged. Only three of the eleven states (Florida, Louisiana, and Virginia) increased population as rapidly as the nation. Two of the three states in America that lost population in the decade were Arkansas and Mississippi. During the years between 1955 and 1960 the rate of out-migration for whites was higher than for nonwhites. Furthermore, whites with the least education predominated in the out-migration.

When such migrants first arrived in cities, they experienced a multitude of problems. Their initial earnings were lower than rural migrants from Midwestern farms who moved to the same cities. Their general adjustment to urban life was also more difficult. In Indianapolis, Indiana, for instance, black migrants from the South were preferred because employers believed rural whites demonstrated less job stability. Southern black migrants were accepted within the local black community, whereas Southern white migrants were not easily assimilated into the larger white community. Even though whites had an easier racial adjustment with the passing years, blacks had an easier initial adjustment.

The Failure of Unionism

Other poor whites became internal migrants, leaving the tenant farm for Southern factories. Although their economic status often improved, many Southern industrial workers in low wage industries did not rise above the government definition of poverty.

The American labor movement tried to assist such workers, but bitter opposition and internal squabbling limited its effectiveness. Both the AFL and the CIO launched major organizing campaigns in the South during 1946. Where their organizing efforts were successful, wages improved and many poor whites joined the lower middle class; and even where such efforts failed, companies oftentimes improved salaries and benefits in an attempt to avoid unionization.

The major CIO–AFL failure came among unskilled and semiskilled workers, especially in the textile industry, precisely those groups that stood at the bottom of the industrial ladder. Conversely, labor successes were scored among more affluent, skilled workers. Even unionism contributed to the distorted image of white poverty. By boasting of its victories and winning substantial benefits for the upper echelon of workers, it obscured the real poverty that persisted among less skilled laborers.

The weakness of Southern unionism can be attributed to social, political, and economic forces. Rural individualism made Southerners hard to organize. The paternalism resulting from close personal relationships caused workers to feel more comfortable with a Southern boss than with an outside labor organizer. Also, rural poverty was so grim and emaciating that the Southern worker would accept factory conditions that laborers in other regions considered intolerable. Racism permeated the region and further divided working-class people. Many poor white workers felt ties of race so strongly that the possibility of joining an integrated union to make common cause against a white owner was unthinkable.

Institutional religion was another hindrance to unionism. As Baptist, Methodist, and Presbyterian laymen entered the middle class, they discarded the concerns that had made many of them reformers in the Populist and Progressive eras. Ministers became better educated, and fewer of them were bivocational, earning a living by farming, in mill or mine, while also pastoring a church. The deacons, stewards, and elders who governed congregations were drawn from the most successful parishioners and dampened the enthusiasm of the occasional minister whose social consciousness challenged the economic order.

Within denominations, class differences persisted between poor congregations in mill-town and middle-class "uptown churches." Middle-class and affluent evangelicals were uncomfortable around their lint-head brethren. People in the mill churches felt equally uneasy in meetings with their coreligionists and sometimes resented middle-class dominance of associational and district affairs. Despite their differences, mill churches hardly threatened the prevalent economic arrangements more than uptown churches; many mill-town congregations worshipped in churches donated by owners who also subsidized the preacher's salary. Paternalistic owners of mines and mills often were respected by workers as godly men genuinely interested in the religious welfare of their employees. No doubt many of them also believed, whether consciously or unconsciously, that religion was an effective method of social control that made their workers sober, reliable, and more content with their fate.

Despite its generally conservative influence, evangelical Christianity continued to prick the social conscience and promote the welfare of workers, just as it had in the 1930s. The ethics of Christ contained the potential to promote upheaval. Lucy Randolph Mason, a pioneer CIO organizer, so challenged the Southern Baptist Convention that it adopted a resolution favoring collective bargaining. Pastor Charles R. Bell of the Parker Memorial Baptist Church in Anniston, Alabama, advanced a number of controversial proposals in the 1930s and 1940s. A member of the Oxford Movement, Bell favored labor reform, unionism, conducted interracial meetings, tried to organize a collective among the poor, became a pacifist, and was finally forced from his pulpit in the mid-1940s.

A more important function of evangelical churches was the training ground they provided the common people in speaking and leadership skills. Evangelical hymnology, its ethics, and democratic church procedure, all influenced Southern unionism. Although some Southern Protestants argued that CIO really stood for "Christ Is Out," Lucy Randolph Mason persuaded many ministers to promote the union. At a 1949 Atlanta conference, the CIO proclaimed that its campaign to organize Southern workers would be "a spiritual crusade led by men with religion in their hearts," a fight to implement the teachings of Christ in the industrial order.

Although union organizers occasionally found allies in the church, they seldom encountered them at the local courthouse. Southern newspapermen and local politicians came primarily from the middle and upper classes and strongly opposed unionism. The right-to-work movement sought to forbid agreements restricting employment to union members and was strongest in the South. Businessmen were not convinced that markets mattered more to new industry than unorganized, cheap labor, and they generally supported anti-union politicians. Union rivalry played into the hands of such politicians, as did the conservatism of the McCarthy era when many politicians equated atheism and communism with membership in the CIO.

Economic factors also inhibited unionism. Many industrial workers in textiles, mining, and timber remained below the income level established as the poverty standard, but a rapid increase in wages between 1940 and 1955 caused them to wonder if unions were necessary. People compared present income to their past experience, not to income of people in other regions doing the same work. Also, the exodus of poor whites from farms to factories provided an available pool of nonunion labor, which threatened their jobs, if they went on strike. The South's five basic industries—textiles, food products, lumber and wood products, apparel, and chemicals—employed large numbers of women who were harder to organize. These industries were in a fragile competitive position with Northern factories, and to maintain their edge, they fought harder to prevent unions. Also, low wages made it more difficult for Southern workers to pay union dues or survive during a strike.

Manufacturing prosperity, automation, unionism, out-migration, wartime prosperity, improvements in health and education—all of these reduced the extent of white poverty following the bleak but publicity-filled days of the depression. By reducing their numbers and by isolating them into pockets surrounded by zones of prosperity, it was easy to forget the poor who remained. The distance from Atlanta to Appalachia was short; but it could be measured in light years during the 1940s and '50s.

Rediscovery

The optimistic notion that poverty all but disappeared as a result of New Deal programs and wartime economic growth had little basis in fact. Even if the number of poor Americans declined by two-thirds between 1936 and 1960, an optimistic estimate made by demographers, this only made the remaining millions more invisible. Several events attracted public attention back to this submerged minority in the early 1960s. As in the 1930s, change began when mainstream Americans gained a new perception of Southern poverty.

Senator John F. Kennedy superficially seemed an unlikely person to befriend Southern poor whites. Son of an affluent New England family, far removed from Southern poverty by education, residence, and culture, he nonetheless played a role in the new antipoverty initiative. This metamorphosis began in the 1960 West Virginia primary when the senator learned as much about local people as they learned about him. The grinding poverty of the Appalachian coal belt surprised and shocked him.

The American intellectual community contributed to Kennedy's education. John Kenneth Galbraith's *The Affluent Society* discussed two categories of disinheritance. "Insular poverty" consisted of large pockets of privation within a generally prosperous land, such as the rural South, West Virginia, and the Ozarks. "Case poverty" included those who were poor because of circumstance rather than location: people with mental deficiencies, bad health, alcoholics, the elderly, the poorly educated. In 1962 Michael Harrington's *The Other America: Poverty in the United States* appeared. Written from a leftist perspective (Harrington served in the 1970s as chairman of the Democratic Socialist Organizing Committee of New York City), the volume was a searing indictment of capitalism and a revelation to all who believed

Family of William Tengle, Alabama sharecroppers, 1936.

The following photographs are by Walker Evans.
Farm Security Administration Collection, Library of Congress.

Ida Ruth Tengle, Alabama, 1936.

Othel "Queekie" Lee Burrough, Alabama, 1936.

Laura Minnie Lee Tengle, Alabama, 1936.

William Tengle, Alabama, 1936.

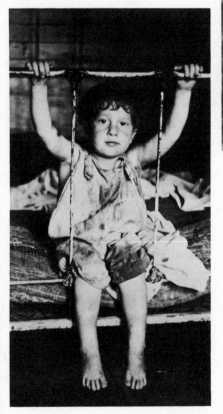

William Fields, Alabama, 1936.

Bud Fields and his family, Alabama sharecroppers, 1936.

that government programs had resolved the problem of indigence in America.

Dwight MacDonald wrote a masterful synthesis of the literature on poverty for *The New Yorker* magazine in January 1963. Entitled "Our Invisible Poor," the article concluded that the number of families with incomes of less than $1,000 annually had actually increased from 800,000 to 1,000,000 between 1953 and 1960. The poor suffered from worse health, possessed less insurance, and paid more taxes in proportion to their income than did the rich. The poorest blacks, farm workers, and isolated rural whites found little relief within the welfare bureaucracy. Constructing a composite from the studies of Harrington and others, MacDonald estimated that between thirty-five and forty million Americans lived in poverty. One presidential advisor claimed that the federal campaign to eliminate poverty in America began when White House assistant Theodore Sorensen showed President Kennedy MacDonald's article in *The New Yorker*. The article documented and confirmed what Kennedy had observed firsthand in West Virginia.

Definition of the nature and extent of poverty quickly became a priority of the New Frontier. In 1964 the Council of Economic Advisers, applying a yardstick of annual family incomes of $3,000 or less, concluded that one-fifth of America's 47 million families were poor. More than half these indigent families had annual incomes below $2,000. Twenty-two percent of the poor were black, a figure representing half the country's Negro population. The poorest families were black, Indian, Puerto Rican, and Mexican American, and the poorest region was the South. Nearly half of all Southern families fell below the $3,000 range, compared to one-fourth of those in the North Central region, 17 percent in the Northeast, and 11 percent in the Western states. Divided according to race, there were three million poor white families in thirteen Southern states in 1966.

The President's National Advisory Commission on Rural Poverty summarized the crisis in remarkably simple, declarative prose: "Most of the rural South is one vast poverty area." The South's population was still disproportionately rural. More than sixty percent of the population of two states lived in nonmetropolitan areas; over fifty percent of three others was rural; in five states more than forty percent; thirty percent in another, and more than twenty-five percent in each of the two remaining states. Most black and white indigents lived in the country but were not farmers. Galbraith's concept of insular poverty was applied to the South where major concentrations of poverty existed in Appalachia, the Ozark Plateau, the South Texas border area, and the Mississippi Delta.

The War on Poverty

What made such statistics startling was the network of government programs that had already been established to eliminate precisely this kind of poverty. To deal with such conditions, additional programs were inaugurated. Both the older programs and the new initiatives fit one of four basic federal strategies: the "aggregationist" approach by which broad fiscal and monetary policies attempted to maintain a high level of economic growth and employment; an "alleviative strategy" which sought to relieve hardships by short- or long-term aid such as unemployment compensation, Medicare, and public assistance; the "curative strategy," using regional development, work training, vocational education, and literacy programs to make the poor self-supporting; the "equal opportunity" philosophy that tried to eliminate discrimination, primarily against racial minorities.

Some programs already existed in the early 1960s. The Area Redevelopment Act, twice vetoed by President Eisenhower, finally passed in 1961. It provided a four-year program of federal assistance for depressed areas where unemployment was persistently above average. The program was not successful. Many economists and politicians blamed its failure on its theory of granting long-term low interest loans to businessmen and the high level of politics involved in its administration. It was allowed to expire in 1965.

The Manpower Training and Development Act of 1962 fell within the curative pattern. It provided loans and grants for job training, was consistent with America's self-help philosophy, and won broad endorsement. It was extended in 1963 and again in 1965, almost without opposition. Twelve Southern states (including Kentucky) accounted for twenty-four percent of total enrollees in the program in 1966, and whites participated in larger numbers than their proportion of the total population.

The Economic Opportunity Act of 1964, which created the Job Corps, Neighborhood Youth Corps, Work-Study, and Head Start, reached a more multiracial audience. This was one of its liabilities insofar as many whites were concerned. Many of the whites who enrolled in the Job Corps were rural people unaccustomed to close association with blacks. When they arrived at training facilities, they encountered large numbers of urban blacks who seemed more aggressive and militant than blacks they had known in the country. Many poor whites, especially in North Carolina, returned home after a few days in Job Corps programs.

Nor did the situation inevitably improve when the programs were brought to whites on the land. Volunteers in Service to America—VISTA—provided work to many idealistic young people in social service agencies. Unfortunately, many of the young were unprepared to understand the culture they confronted. Coming from middle- and upper-class families, well educated, and rather secular, they were unsympathetic to fundamentalist religion and rejected the fatalism that they encountered. Many poor whites accepted whatever specific assistance they offered, but resented the air of smug superiority that often accompanied it. The most successful VISTA volunteers were those who discovered that they had as much to learn from the poor as they had to teach.

Another major federal initiative was the Economic Development Act of 1965, which provided a five-year 3.25-billion-dollar program of grants and loans for economic assistance to depressed areas. The act combined features of three previous programs—the Area Redevelopment Act, the Accelerated Public Works Act of 1962, and the Appalachian Regional Development Act of 1965. It financed public works programs such as water and sewer systems, road and airport construction, and provided for multistate regional planning commissions. In fact, one of the most notable features of the poverty program was its acceptance of regionalism as a basic approach.

As the New Deal had once before emphasized the problem South, the 1960s War On Poverty refocused attention on the section. The 1930s regionalism of Howard Odum and Rupert Vance had in some ways been essentially conservative, despite its emphasis on regional planning. Odum had depicted American culture as an amalgamation of traditions that were bound to the land and to folk society. His emphasis upon the interrelationship of land-people-culture had challenged the cosmopolitan urbanism of that time. The vitality of American life, Odum thought, was rooted in the soil, and regionalism sought national renovation through the orderly development of human resources on the regional level. The mobility of Americans in the years after World War II resulted in so much migration between sections that Odum's regionalism seemed less relevant. Returning prosperity and a revolution in communications further eroded local identification with a sense of place, and fostered loyalty to a unified culture.

The rediscovery of poverty provoked a reappraisal of regionalism. It became apparent in the 1960s that poverty "pockets" actually were not pockets at all, but were large, contiguous areas. The neoregionalism that resulted from this discovery lacked the cultural idealism of Howard Odum and was more narrowly economic in focus. Poverty was defined in simpler economic terms, and combatants in the war were far less interested in the culture of the poor.

The most far-reaching example of neoregionalism was the creation of the Appalachian Regional Commission in 1965, an event which will be discussed more fully in the final chapter. It inspired other planning groups, which focused on the Ozarks, New England, the Great Lakes, and the Great Plains.

The diagnosis of Appalachian ills was followed by a broader study in 1967 by the National Advisory Committee on Rural Poverty. Whereas the Economic Opportunity Act of 1964 had aimed at the elimination of urban poverty, the new investigation examined the fourteen million rural poor. Of these, eleven million were white with the majority concentrated in the South. Problem areas in addition to Appalachia included the Ozarks, the heavily black Coastal Plain, and the Mexican-American border area of the Southwest. Most of the rural poor were not farmers; instead, they lived in nonfarm rural areas. In both conception and proposed remedy, the Rural Advisory Committee was more adventurous than the Appalachian Commission had been. Its definition of poverty extended beyond income levels. Poor education, lack of jobs, lack of access to status positions, insecurity, unstable homes, and the lack of political power necessary to improve their own lives all contributed to a wretched existence that perpetuated indigence from one generation of the rural poor to the next.

The committee's report was a powerful indictment entitled *The People Left Behind*. It documented hunger, high rates of disease, early death, a rural unemployment rate sometimes as high as eighteen percent, poor education, and housing. The South's rural poor had been denied participation in Social Security until the 1950s, and they still lacked unemployment insurance, the right of collective bargaining, and workmen's compensation. To eliminate urban poverty without lifting rural blight was self-defeating and would only siphon millions more of the rural poor into the city.

America possessed the resources to eliminate rural poverty but lacked the will. Among commission proposals were: guarantee of full employment, including federal creation of jobs if the private sector could not absorb the entire labor force; expansion of public assistance and food stamp programs; manpower development aimed at the indigent; better preschool education; and rent supplements.

The report attracted mixed reaction. The editor of *Fortune* magazine remembered that much of the opposition to the Appalachian Act had come from conservative Southern Democrats and wondered if the report had not ignored the most critical problem of the rural poor, namely, white Southern officials and their cohorts who controlled American agricultural policy. The editor argued that the Department of Agriculture had devoted more energy to fighting the erosion of soil than stemming the erosion of people. The American Farm Bureau

Federation, in fact, had been as active as the Chamber of Commerce and the National Association of Manufacturers in battling antipoverty programs for the rural poor.

Whether these programs have operated sufficiently long to provide insights into their success or failure is dubious. Inflation, unemployment, and crime quickly usurped poverty as fashionable concerns for congressmen and state legislators, and the life expectancy of poverty programs has never been long. Consequently, such programs must accomplish whatever they intend quickly.

Victories in the War on Poverty

The intent of all such programs was noble and there were individual successes. Public works projects provided temporary employment, and job training offered the promise of more permanent solutions. Idealistic volunteers improved community life, and depressed areas were assisted at least temporarily by the infusion of federal funds. But most of this aid was aimed at economic problems, and most of its conveyors had limited experience in working with Southern poor whites. Many of the assumptions on which poverty programs were based applied to urban whites and blacks better than to rural folk. Perhaps Americans also overestimated the capacity of "programs" to alter the conditions of individuals. The culture of poor people provided them with certain compensations for their poverty—freedom to fish and hunt whenever they pleased, less pressure and less orientation of their lives—and this culture was not so amenable to change as more affluent people seemed to expect.

Although the pace of progress left almost everyone dissatisfied, conditions among the Southern poor did improve. Employment rose slowly, welfare rolls declined, and not as many people left the land; new hospitals, roads, parks, water and sewer systems were built.

Some of this improvement was attributable to various government programs, but a large amount of private industrial development also occurred in rural counties during the 1960s. Many geographers and economists argued that poverty could be solved only by relocating the rural poor into intermediate-sized cities. During the 1960s, however, industry seemed to be going to the country. Within the thirteen-state area there was a 48.9 percent increase in nonfarm jobs in rural counties. Rural counties in Alabama, Tennessee, South Carolina, and Arkansas had unusually high rates of increase in manufacturing employment. For the first time in history, manufacturing jobs outnumbered farm employment in rural counties of Mississippi, South Carolina, and Arkansas. Industries, which made machinery and transportation equipment, locating in rural areas paid higher salaries than the textile mills that had preceded them. This trend challenged two widely held hypotheses: first, that it was nearly impossible for rural communities to attract industry; secondly, that industry that located in rural areas was inevitably low wage and exploitative. The nature of rural industrialization in the 1960s, its relatively higher wage structure, the possibility it offered for employing a second, usually female, family member, helped many rural folk to stay in the country and made a positive contribution to the general welfare of the South.

Skirmishes were won on many fronts. The most notable gains were in overwhelmingly white counties in the Ozarks and Appalachia. One evidence of substantial improvement in the economic welfare of Southern poor whites was the stabilizing of white population. During the years from 1970 to 1973 only Alabama, Louisiana, and Mississippi showed decreases in population due to out-migration. Among states notable for losing poor whites over the previous three decades, Arkansas and Kentucky registered gains.

Defeats in the War on Poverty

Despite these achievements, poor whites remained in the South in significant numbers. In 1959, 40 million Americans (22 percent of the population) had family incomes so low as to qualify them for the poverty level; by 1968 the total had declined to 25.4 million, or 13 percent of the population. But after 1968 the number of poor people remained relatively constant. At the end of 1971 their numbers had risen slightly to 25.5 million (12.5 percent). Of these, 44 percent lived in the South, and 70 percent of the Southern poor were white. According to the 1970 census, 3.4 million, 58.8 percent, of the poor living in the rural South were white. The South—including Kentucky, Oklahoma, and West Virginia—was the only region of America in the 1970 census where a majority of the white poor lived in rural, nonfarm areas.

Such people had been neglected because of the popular assumptions that Southern rural poverty was mainly limited to blacks, that it primarily involved farmers, and that regional economic growth would eliminate it. None of this had happened by 1970. In fact, between 1959 and 1969 the Southern white share of total American rural poverty actually increased slightly. Poverty programs of the 1960s, though designed to reach all the poor, had not effectively reached whites. The result was that Southern poor whites were more deeply alienated from the national mainstream than any ethnic group.

A 1970s profile of Southern poor whites revealed predictable as well as surprising information. They were older and more poorly educated than the average Southerner. Most of them were employed in low-wage jobs; among heads of families, 51 percent worked forty hours or more per week without escaping poverty. Furthermore, such folk did not receive a proportionate share of public assistance expenditures provided by federal, state, and local sources.

The profile must also include the dismal condition of health care for poor whites. The poor residing in rural areas faced special health hazards. Four contributing factors to the health care crisis of the 1970s were lower income, higher percentages of elderly people, lower educational levels, and a general shortage of medical personnel. In December 1971, forty-seven counties in the former Confederacy had no practicing physician at all. In 1972, of Mississippi's 82 counties, 65 contained no pediatrician, 59 no obstetric/gynecologist, 45 no general surgeon. Conditions were as bad in Arkansas and Alabama and only slightly better in other Southern states. Not even the right to health, much less to liberty and happiness, belonged equally to all Southerners.

Future projections by economists forecast a continuation of

wretched conditions for low-income farm families. The greatest decline in farm employment will occur in those areas where income is already lowest. Although a higher percentage of the South's nonwhite population falls within the bottom economic range, the implications are the same for whites with low incomes. They must look to nonfarm jobs, mainly in the cities, because they have no long-range future in Southeastern agriculture. Perhaps Southern economic growth will absorb a higher proportion of the region's poor into its own cities, but many will continue to migrate north, making this a national problem.

Many proposals have been advanced to ameliorate the problem of out-migration. Vocational education for farm youth should emphasize skills that have a broader applicability than solely agriculture. Many of the young will leave for urban industrial jobs. In fact, more than half the graduates of vocational agricultural and 4-H programs will find nonfarm jobs. Also, they need some basic social skills to allow them to understand and cope with urban ways of life. Another critical need is a more efficient method of transmitting employment information. Migration is effective only if it occurs between areas that have surplus population and regions that experience labor shortages. A third method of absorbing the rural poor, more rapid industrial growth in the Southeast, is the most promising development of the 1970s.

Good Old Boys

Charts and graphs portray the economics of poverty and are important; but statistical tables depict only part of the experience of being poor. Southern poor whites were not only economically different from upper-class whites, they also maintained a unique subculture. Part of the reason for the rediscovery of Southern white poverty in the 1960s was the interest that the nation took in this different way of life.

One of the most enduring fixtures of Southern society was the "Good Old Boy." Part redneck, part practical genius, the good old boy belonged to a world of moonshining, modified cars, country music, and Saturday night wrestling. For him, professional baseball or a college football scholarship was a ticket from poverty to the good life.

He enthroned his own hero whom he identified in his own way (a "hell-of-a-good-fellow").

In the 1950s and 1960s the class lines began to blur as stock car racing, country music, evangelical religion, and blatant racism began to appeal to other sections and classes; but the poor white subculture had its own special claims on all these. Before auto racing became the highly organized, expensive sport of the 1970s, it was a Saturday or Sunday afternoon extension of the wild drive out of the hills with a load of illicit whiskey. Eddy Arnold popularized country music by making it velvet smooth, but it began with twanging banjo and nasal whine. Racism was by no means exclusively Southern poor white by the 1970s, but the American public associated the most blatant and violent racism with this class.

The most negative stereotype of Southern poor white subculture centered on race. As with many stereotypes, this one had much evidence to support it. In 1973 Jessie L. Thrift of Semmes was a minor candidate for governor of Alabama. His campaign lacked the catchy slogans designed by well-paid public relations firms; he called himself "A Rebel for Christ" and "The Hanging Candidate for Governor." His attacks on Jews and blacks culminated in a pledge to try integrationist federal judges before a "Christian Posse" and hang them. His autobiography constituted a disturbing catalogue of the crippling psychological baggage of poor white poverty even for those who had obtained middle-class status:

> Youngest child of a family of fifteen children
> Son of a share-cropper
> Grandson of a Confederate soldier
> Quit school in the 6th grade to help out at home
> Went to work in a cotton-mill when I was 13 years
> 　　old as a lint-head
> I ran whiskey out of the Smokey Mountains in North
> 　　Carolina and Tennessee
> Joined the Army in 1950, a week after my 16th birthday
> Decorated five times
> Platoon Sargent in the Combat Infantry in Korea when
> 　　I was 18 years old

Served four years and was honorably discharged
Took up the trade of brick masonry and became a
     successful masonry contractor which business
     spanned five "Southern States"
Joined the Ku-Klux-Klan in 1959 to help save my
     race
Father of five children, all of them thoroughbreds.
     Adopted three nephews and raised them to manhood.
     One of them, Freddie, died in the Marines in
     Viet Nam. Frank and Willie are now serving
     honorably in the Navy.

This is my background in brief, I offer no apologies
or excuses for any of it. I want my final epitaph
to read; and this will be my legacy to my children:
"He was a Naturalborn Rebel and he tried". . . .
Then it would all have been worthwile.[1]

The results of such racism have been all too obvious: one-sided justice, demagogic politics, educational and economic discrimination, and mindless violence, all of this supported by substantial numbers of Southern whites whose main source of pride was their race. One 1950s example was Guilford County, North Carolina, where income and resistance to desegregation were closely related. Hard-core resistance, defined as the willingness to use force to resist change, came mostly from whites with annual mean incomes of 3,500 dollars or less. The hard-core resisters were slightly younger than the general population, belonged to the same churches as other whites and in about the same proportions, attended church as frequently, and were as stable in residence patterns. The ways in which resisters differed from the general population were most important: they were more concentrated in rural areas, their earning power was significantly less, few were white-collar professionals, and they were less educated. Because they possessed few of the tools necessary to improve their lives—education, income, and prestige occupations—they rested at the bottom of the white social structure and were most threatened by upward black mobility.

The response of Southern poor whites to the federal economic reform programs of the 1960s seemed to confirm the persistence of racism among poor whites. Since many poverty programs represented the federal response to racial inequities publicized by the civil rights movement, Southern poor whites often refused to participate in them. The response of indigent whites to activities of the Office of Economic Opportunity in Craven County, North Carolina, was typical. The mostly rural east coast county was the site of the historic colonial capital of New Bern and in 1960 was the home of 2,772 poor white families and 2,360 poor black ones. The first OEO program began in 1964. From the beginning, poor whites shunned these efforts, refused to acknowledge their own poverty, and emphasized their kinship with middle-class whites. When community leaders condemned poverty projects as socialistic, many low-income whites preferred not to participate rather than lose the respect of more affluent neighbors. When OEO leaders insisted that blacks be given equal access to antipoverty programs, they effectively eliminated Caucasians from participation. The result was that poor whites were even more alienated from society than were local blacks. The same pattern existed throughout most of the state. North Carolina contained more poor people than any other Southern state, some 234,000 families of whom sixty-six percent were white; yet, relatively few whites participated in federal antipoverty programs.

Southern politics demonstrated the tremendous impact of race on poor whites. A coalition of white farmers and urban working-class whites and blacks had united behind economic liberals in the 1930s and 1940s to elect men such as Claude Pepper and Lister Hill, but race became more important than economic reform during the 1950s and 1960s. Although national attention focused on the newly enfranchised black voters, the greatest increase in voter participation during the 1960s was among less-educated whites. White people with less than a high school education, who held blue-collar jobs, and belonged to the lower-income level, voted in record numbers.

Although many lower-income whites deserted the Democratic party, they did not necessarily vote Republican. They characterized themselves as independents, and their favorite candidates were regional Democrats, especially Lester G. Maddox of Georgia and George C. Wallace of Alabama. Running under the banner of the American Independent party in the 1968 presidential election, Wallace swept low-income white precincts against both Republican and Democratic opponents.

The Wallace vote in 1968 was essentially a protest vote against national trends largely confined to presidential politics. Since the Republican party did not benefit on the state or local level from poor white defection from the Democratic party, it was uncertain where the lower-income white vote would go in the 1970s. It was obvious that poor whites had changed their emphasis between 1956 and 1968, and that change had influenced their party loyalty. In 1956 large majorities of blacks and whites favored the idea of a federal guarantee of jobs, whereas by 1968 Southern whites of all classes overwhelmingly opposed such a philosophy. The late 1960s seemed to indicate that lower-income whites shared the economic attitudes of affluent whites rather than more liberal blacks. Ironically, poor whites opposed candidates who had been instrumental in passing poverty programs to help them. Class-based politics seemed a casualty of the civil rights movement as poor whites ignored economic grievances and focused on retaining white supremacy.

Then came the statewide elections of 1970 and 1971 when a number of moderate Southern Democrats attracted poor white support to win senatorial and gubernatorial offices. In Louisiana, for instance, Governor Edwin Edwards won solid backing from both urban blacks and rural poor whites.

Other instances of interracial economic cooperation demonstrated reduced tension. During the late 1960s two Appalachian-based organizations, the Black Lung Association and the Disabled Miners and Widows, began pressuring unions and mine operators for reforms. The two organizations were led by black West Virginia coal miners Charles Brooks and Robert Payne, but the membership of both was biracial.

Mississippi was the setting for another biracial organization of poor people, the Gulfcoast Pulpwood Association. In the 1970s nearly two-thirds of the nation's pulp products originated along the shorelines and inland pine forests of Georgia, Alabama, Mississippi, Louisiana, and North Florida. Most of the cutting and hauling was done by some 200,000 independent truck owners who were about equally divided between blacks and whites. Many were only years removed from sharecropping and their incomes were often below the poverty line. In the fall of 1971 the Gulfcoast Pulpwood Association's six thousand members went on strike. The membership, though sixty percent black, maintained solidarity and won some concessions.

But such biracial organizations were only a beginning. Racial discrimination influenced the attitudes and institutions of the white poor as well as those of blacks. A long history of racial segregation within churches, housing, politics, unions, and industry left poor whites less able to recognize and confront discrimination than blacks. Also, poor whites did not develop a common identification and were therefore more isolated, lacked effective leadership, and had no constructive causes to advocate. Only in the negative sense of stopping the progress of Negroes did they sometimes feel commonality.

Evangelical religion was a second aspect of poor white life to be negatively stereotyped. Culture-bound Southern folk religion cut across denominational lines to form a conservative, frequently emotional, fundamentalist subculture. Even though Southern poor whites often neglected formal church membership, they were nevertheless devotedly religious. Yet, the prejudice against their sectarianism has been so strong that few scholars have explored this underside of American religion.

The value system that provided poor whites a sense of worth was as complicated as their racial views. Among poor white sects—the Church of Christ, Church of God of Apostolic Faith, Church of God, New Testament Holiness Church, Church of God of Prophecy, and others—one finds diverse social and racial views. Sect leaders became the spokesmen of inarticulate common folk in much the same way that George Wallace became their political leader. They spoke the mind of people who controlled no other institutions through which they could make their desires known.

The sects were not exclusively apolitical, withdrawn, and other-worldly. On the contrary, they sometimes reacted aggressively to social problems. In fact, the boldest religious challenge to Southern racism came from the most extreme of the Pentecostal sects rather than from middle-class denominations; the most thoroughly integrated church in the South between 1945 and the mid-1960s was the Church of God of Prophecy.

The key to unraveling this paradox is to be found in the class struc-ture of evangelicals. Decades ago sociologist Max Weber noted that the privileged required religion to reassure them of the legitimacy of things as they are. The poor replaced what they could not be now with what they would become later. The lower the social class, the more radical were the forms assumed by its savior. Although serious theo-logical issues divided older denominations ("churches") and newer sects, social class played as critical a role. Evangelical religion, like country music, sometimes crossed the color line to appeal to poor blacks and whites alike.

Perhaps this explained the remarkable ministry of Will Campbell, a Southern Baptist minister who repudiated the liberal theology he encountered at Yale and who chose to live in a log cabin near Nash-ville, where he ministered to the poor of both races during the tumul-tuous 1960s. Born on a forty-acre cotton farm in Mississippi, he be-came an activist in the civil rights movement long before such involve-ment became fashionable. He distrusted institutions, believing that no matter how good their intentions, they magnified the estrangement be-tween people. His individualistic, unorthodox attempt to change hearts seemed strange until a more urbane secular culture began to wrestle with the reality that laws rarely established even justice, much less brotherhood. His lonely voice crying in the wilderness began to sound more prophetic than lunatic.

An event in 1974 in West Virginia emphasized the need for Camp-bell's variety of wisdom on issues other than race. White fundamental-ists in Kanawha County, West Virginia, burned textbooks that of-fended their religious beliefs and ignored their deeply held values. Americans reacted with more emotion than understanding. Such an act seemed to strike at the heart of the educational process. Yet in their own way these angry parents were saying the same thing a mountain boy had told a pioneer missionary: "Bring us your civilization, but leave us our own culture." Their culture had served them well against a hostile environment and exploitative economics. Self-sufficient people who found their own kind of meaning and happiness in life (it was not necessary that all agreed on the meaning or the happiness), resented being told that the price they must pay for progress, even survival, was the loss of their culture.

One aspect of poor white subculture fared better than its racial views and religion. By mid-century country music enjoyed a national following, and Ryman Hall in Nashville, Tennessee, was its capital. Located in central Tennessee midway between the mountains of Knoxville and the Mississippi flatlands of Memphis, Nashville symbolized the connection between rural Appalachia and urban America. The music that came from Ryman was both more and less than country music.

Tom Ryman, for whom the Grand Ole Opry house was named, was a hard-living riverboat operator who was "saved" in the late nineteenth century. In gratitude he built a downtown tabernacle of brick and stained glass, which reverberated initially to the sermons of Billy Sunday and other evangelists. Although the Opry dated from 1925, it did not move into the Ryman permanently until 1943. The move was logical, for many of the same folk who had constituted Sunday's audience came to hear Hank Snow, Roy Acuff, and Sam McGee. Those of less religious persuasion left the Opry headed for Tootsie's Orchid Lounge across the alley from Ryman, where truck drivers fraternized with country music stars in ribald egalitarianism.

Even if the color line long prevailed at Tootsie's, the music crossed racial boundaries. The lament of Negro and white seemed to have a commonality, epitomized by black harmonica player DeFord Bailey, the first man known to have made a record in Nashville and an early Opry star. Despite its cliquishness and commercialization, the Opry popularized some of the best mountain musicians such as Louis Marshall (Grandpa) Jones. Jones, born in a rural Kentucky community, employed his five-string banjo and droll wit to link folksong and country music genres and popularized them at the Opry.

By 1972 country music was no longer the province of rural America. That year country music accounted for twenty-six percent of all sales at Columbia Records, and the percentage went up in 1973. The Nashville Sound had become an institution, and it also had departed from its poor white mountain/country origins. The last performance of the Opry at old Ryman Hall on March 15, 1974, was a belated epitaph. The crowd consisted mainly of white folks, many of whom had escaped poverty but who had retained poor white culture. Johnny Cash led the entire cast in an old melody popularized by the Carter family, which had become the Opry's theme song: "Will the Circle Be Unbroken?" Jimmy Snow, son of the legendary Hank Snow, preached a final fire and brimstone sermon, and many a wet-eyed participant filed out of the old hall.

The next night the Opry moved to a slick new amusement park in a Nashville suburb. The audience included Nashville business people who recognized the commercial potential of Opryland. The audience also contained congressmen, three governors, two United States senators, and President Richard Nixon. The President praised country music for its references to family, religion, and love of country as a reflection of the heart of America.

The evening was symbolic of what mainstream America could do to distort Southern poor white culture. Country music had long since lost its purity and innocence, but the tribute paid it by Richard Nixon was a final irony. Ballads whose lyrics likely as not spoke of divorce, infidelity, seduction, sung by sleazy peroxided blondes in a thousand honkytonks, became moral lessons. An idiom that had served Harlan County coal miners and redneck ne'er-do-wells who loved George Wallace became a tribute to the values of Middle America. The music and verse, the original performers and their historic audience, were not quintessential America; they were poor Southern whites who for most of their history had been ignored or caricatured by the very same Middle America they suddenly were supposed to symbolize.

Southern poor whites experienced as cataclysmic change after

World War II as most other minorities, although the nation was less aware of them. Americans assumed that the New Deal programs directed at the poor and postwar prosperity would eliminate this minority. The 1960s rediscovery of poverty in America demonstrated how naive this assumption was. The rediscovery led to yet another federal war on poverty, with similarly disheartening results.

The difficulties inherent in improving the economic conditions of poor whites were complicated by their own racism and by negative attitudes toward them. Many citizens stereotyped them as otherworldly religious fanatics and redneck racists. Whatever solutions emerged in future years, the decade and a half following John Kennedy's West Virginia campaign was instructive. It was much easier to forget poverty than to conceive imaginative proposals to eliminate it. Even if local political inequity and racism had played significant roles in white poverty, the elimination of all these barriers might not resolve the crisis. Any proposed solution must recognize unique problems that exist among Southern whites, including cultural isolation and racism bred by ignorance, fear, and powerlessness. To engineer programs that ignore unique regional culture will only retrace the well-traveled road that relegated millions of Southerners to another generation of unfulfilled promises and continued poverty.

CHAPTER SIX

APPALACHIAN SPRING— AND WINTER

Chancellor Joseph C. Smiddy of Clinch Valley College, Wise, Virginia, has spent his life collecting mountain stories and music. One of his tales contains much wisdom. In the early 1970s six feet of snow buried Wise and the surrounding hills. After snow remained on the ground for nearly six weeks, the local rescue squad became concerned over the fate of Granny Jane Collins, who lived alone in a log cabin on High Knob. Snow plows and bulldozers feverishly labored to clear a path to Granny Collins' door. Rescue workers anxiously knocked, only to be greeted by a sprightly and obviously perturbed woman who announced: "I contributed to you-uns last summer." Like so many Appalachian folk, Granny Collins did not realize she needed rescuing.

Economic, geographical, and political isolation all contributed to the fierce individualism of Granny Collins and other Appalachian people. Historically and culturally they deviated in important ways from other Southerners. Slavery was never important to the economy of the hill people in the antebellum era. During the Civil War, they were divided in their loyalties, perhaps producing as many recruits for Northern armies as for Southern. Following the Civil War, Appalachian counties tended to vote Republican in opposition to the Democratic vote of other Southern whites. Although Appalachian poor whites shared much in common with their lowland neighbors, the differences between them justify their separate treatment.

Appalachian culture posed even more fundamental difficulties than political history for Americans interested in resolving the problems of the region. Theoretically, government officials understood the necessity of relating assistance to the unique culture of those who needed help. But Americans have not been successful in offering aid without imposing their mainstream values. Domestic reform programs conceived in the 1960s often ignored the long historical traditions of isolation that date back more than two hundred years. Many theorists who professed concern for the physical welfare of poor whites treated Pentecostal religion, which provided succor for the soul, as a mental aberration to be exorcised as rapidly as possible. The most notable example of mainstream American culture shock occurred in Appalachia where federal largess was met by opposition or indifference. Race played only a minor role in this reaction, but culture produced an equally formidable resistance.

The Historic Setting of Appalachian Poverty

The isolation that helped produce Appalachian poverty dates from the earliest settlement. The traditional definition of the southern Appalachians encompassed 80,000 square miles in parts of seven states. It included three physiographic areas: the Blue Ridge Mountains on the east; the Great Valley in the center; and the Cumberland-Allegheny plateaus on the west. Within Appalachia were three major subgroups sharing distinctive values and behavior patterns: rural mountain folk, coal miners, and small town middle-class people. The first two of these were overwhelmingly poor whites.

The oldest of these groups consisted of rural mountain people. Most early pioneers crossed the eastern front of the mountains in Pennsylvania, followed the valleys south, then turned west through passes such as Cumberland Gap, which allowed them to enter the rich land of the Cumberland and Ohio valleys. But not all settlers continued the trek westward. Some liked the isolation and beauty of remote hollows and hilltops and remained in the mountains. They were ethnically homogeneous, coming mainly from Scotland by way of Ulster and Northern Ireland, and bringing a rich heritage of seventeenth-century British culture with them. The motivation of these mountain folk is debatable. Harry Caudill hypothesized in his provocative book, *Night Comes to the Cumberlands,* that most people who sought the isolation of the mountains were orphans, outlaws, or desperately poor. This origin, he believed, explained the shiftless, lazy, unskilled, and illiterate people of the mountains. Historians dispute this explanation, however, arguing that many of the pioneers were indentured servants, poor but sturdy folk who were searching for new land and a place where they would be left alone. Despite differences between Appalachia and the rest of the South, mountain people shared with other poor whites a sense of pride, fierce independence, a mixture of nostalgia and impatience, bitterness at their fate and yet resignation to it.

Isolation aided in the preservation of the customs and traditions of seventeenth-century Britain and the development of a homogeneous culture that was ninety-five percent white and overwhelmingly rural. Physical access was difficult and offered no advantages to a farmer who could easily pass through Cumberland Gap and homestead in the fertile Bluegrass region. Laurel thickets, heavy brush, canebreaks, poor soil, and steep hills made commercial farming difficult. The result was a land of subsistence farming and dispersed settlement. Settlers learned to provide for themselves: home remedies, homemade furniture, and home brew. The first pioneers located in bottom land along streams, with late arrivals moving farther upstream, and finally onto the hillsides. Soil depletion, erosion, and flooding followed, and poverty seemed to be worse the farther one went up the hollow or toward the branch heads. Communication and travel followed the streams, and directions still are given in relation to a creek or branch.

The mountaineers were isolated both from the outside world and from each other. Family groups were close and clan ties strong. Entire geographical regions were peopled by a family group that had little interest in communicating with surrounding areas. Sometimes the prodigious number of their offspring taxed the resources of their creek or hollow. In 1918 one branch of Troublesome Creek in Kentucky, only three miles long, contained thirteen houses and a total of 96 people, of whom 67 were children. Depletion of game and exhaustion of soil made poverty endemic.

Strong kinship ties provided a basic orientation for rural mountain people. The obligations of an individual to his kin held priority over other individuals or groups. Strangers were suspect. Hostility toward an enemy was equally strong and also was determined by kinship.

American history did not bypass the mountains during the nineteenth century, but the pattern of impact was like an Appalachian valley: full of sudden twists and depressions. The Civil War divided communities, and many mountain people favored the Union. Only rarely did they own slaves, and loyalty to the federal government often was as strong as in any New England township. Except for occasional marauders and skirmishes, the war did not penetrate the remote mountains.

The infamous family feuds of the 1875–1915 period, which contributed so much to the hillbilly stereotype, resulted from such divisions. Although less than one percent of the population of the mountains became involved in the thirteen major feuds, more than one hundred men were killed. The issues varied. Many dated from bitter Civil War arguments; drunken brawls caused others, partly accounting for the growing prohibition sentiment in some areas of the southern Highlands. Sheriffs and judges who administered justice unfairly also played a role. After 1920 only local feuds confined to a single valley or county continued.

Extralegal violence was accepted as part of the moral code among people whose frontier habitation extended beyond the range of legal institutions. Even their subcultural heroes celebrated in story and ballad were likely to be outlaws; murders, especially those involving young women, also found their way into folklore.

During the years of family feuds, chaotic change came to the mountains. One-room common schools were established in the hills, supported by missionary societies, property taxes, and state aid. Economic change was more significant and brought two new subcultures, coal mining and middle-class towns, to compete with rural mountain culture.

Railroads constructed after the Civil War opened the rich coal fields of the Cumberland and Allegheny plateaus, particularly in West Virginia, eastern Kentucky, and southwestern Virginia. Lumbering and coal mining had become important to local economies by the 1890s. The first load of coal was shipped by rail from Wise County, Virginia, in 1892, and from Harlan County, Kentucky, in 1911. The population of Wise County mushroomed from 9,400 in 1890 to 47,000 in 1920. Some of these newcomers were Hungarians, Poles, Greeks, Italians, and Negroes. Most were not. They came up from the hollows and down from the hills in search of a more stable source of income. What followed was a boom-town psychology well described in his romantic novel, *The Trail of the Lonesome Pine,* by John Fox, Jr. The wage system replaced barter and exchange, and the company commissary provided store-bought goods. But the change can be exaggerated. Roads remained poor or nonexistent, and mining communities were economically isolated, made up entirely of miners, their families, and company officials. The grinding poverty of the tiny farms gave way to perpetual debt, payment in company script, and dirty, back-breaking, often deadly underground mining. Isolation was replaced first by the crowded life of the company row houses, and then by the shifting from camp to camp following coal seams and economic cycles.

Industrial Poverty in Appalachia

Coal mining did not open the mountains to mainstream culture; it only fragmented rural mountain culture. The markets, ownership, and control of the coal remained in Pittsburgh, New York, and Chicago. Rail, telephone, and roads connected towns near the camps to the outside world, and they became the residences of chemists, engineers, doctors, lawyers, real estate salesmen, and coal operators. Although most communities remained small, generally 2,000 people or less, social class distinctions unknown to mountain culture became visible. Civic and social clubs, business associations, high schools and hospitals, Episcopal parishes, "uptown" First Baptist and First Methodist churches, marked the emergence of a small middle class amidst remote mountain cabins and isolated mining camps. By 1930 three subcultures, each with its own values and needs, coexisted in relative peace, but not for long.

Armageddon bore a hundred names in the 1930s, but the most famous was Harlan. The county was a primitive Appalachian region as recently as 1910. When the first railroad entered in 1911, there were six coal mines operating. By 1931, there were seventy-one. The number of miners who clawed coal from the bosom of the mountains was 169 in 1910, climbed to 9,260 by 1923, and peaked at over 10,000 just before the depression. Mountaineers who seldom earned one hundred dollars a year heard fantastic tales of steady work, where one could earn more in one month than moonshining and farming brought annually. Coal companies promised free transportation to the camp and decent living quarters with electric lights and running water. Strong, rawboned men came out of the hills with their horde of offspring, swallowed their fears, affixed a carbide lamp to their caps, and entered the blackness. Beneath the ground they squeezed timbers into place, undercut seams of coal, bored holes into the face of coal seams, fixed dynamite charges, "blew it," then returned to load the rock and coal aboard cars, which mules pulled to the surface. Death was commonplace, the greatest danger coming from rock falls and not from the explosions that attracted more public attention only because the immediate toll in life was so great.

When periodic slumps hit the coal market, men were fired. The government had no experience in providing for the rural unemployed, so they went hungry or took their families back up the hollows. In 1932 Harlan County miners had virtually no occupational skills other than mining; 78.2 percent had only an elementary education, and Kentucky ranked forty-seventh among the forty-eight states in rates of literacy. The county was so poor and remote from other kinds of employment that when depression struck, there were few alternatives. The county made little provision for welfare or relief, and these funds were quickly exhausted by the cataclysm that struck in 1929. Within three years coal production was halved, wages fell fifty-eight percent, and three thousand miners lost their jobs. Most of the others worked only two or three day weeks.

Just across Big Black Mountain from Harlan County the mining camp at Stonega, Virginia, nestled beneath the hills. M. C. Sizemore's father took him out of the third grade to help plow two acres that belonged to the Stonega Coal Company. At the age of eighteen Sizemore entered the mines. By the 1930s he was loading four tons on a coal car, and running three cars a day for seventy-six cents a car:

Q. You were working three days a week.

A. I was. What it was, you see, I'd have a cut three days out of the week, you see.

Q. So three days a week you were just getting dirt out and you were not getting paid. . . .

A. Yea, that's right. . . . Back in them days, buddy, it would make you want to do wrong. . . . All the people who lived in this hollow here had about the same thing, too.

. . . .

Well, you had to get okayed script every evening you know . . .

Q. What do you mean by okay script?

A. Well what it was, you see, the superintendent was over the mines, you know, he'd take his pencil . . . he'd charge you [give on credit] a dollar script.

Q. Did the okay script at the end of the day mean that you got that amount of script to use at the company store instead of having to wait till you got to payday?

A. Yea, that's what you had to do to get stuff to pack your bucket with the next day.

Q. And then if you waited till payday they would pay you in money?

A. Yea, what little bit. You know how much money I drawed in four years time when what's his name—Hoover—was in there? I'm ashamed to tell it. Thirty-five cents.

Q. Thirty-five cents! For four years?

A. If that ain't the truth the Man up there knows I am lying.

Q. In actual cash money?

A. Cash. A dime in one statement and a quarter in another one. And I had a notion to throw both of them away.

Q. And the rest of the time you just used script?

A. And the rest of the time I didn't get nothing. Didn't get nothing. Why it was just slavery, what you might call it.[1]

Despite the traditional reluctance of mountain men to cooperate or act to improve their status, six thousand Harlan County miners responded to their poverty by joining the United Mine Workers of America in 1931. Several hundred unionists were discharged, and outraged miners reacted with looting and violence, resulting in the deaths of four mine guards and one miner. The National Guard occupied the county, provoking six thousand miners to walk off their jobs. The UMW withdrew from the inflammatory situation, only to be replaced by the National Mine Workers Union, a Communist rival to the UMW. The decision of individualistic, religious mountain folk to join the NMWU is testimony to the desperation to which poverty and hungry families drove them.

For six years a reign of terror prevailed in Bloody Harlan. No historical incident better demonstrated the powerlessness of poor whites. Local institutions—courts, police, county government, businesses, schools—were dominated by mine owners. Both sheriffs who served the county between 1930 and 1938, John Henry Blair and Theodore Roosevelt Middleton, served the interests of owners. The two county judges were usually submissive. Through their cooperation, 169 deputy sheriffs were appointed, of whom 64 had been indicted and 37 convicted of felonies, 8 for manslaughter and 3 for murder. Deputies dispersed union rallies and intimidated labor organizers.

Many residents of Harlan County blamed the upheaval on union anarchy and believed this justified the use of violence against the miners. One union organizer's apartment was dynamited and two union leaders were wounded in ambushes. A union strategy session was interrupted by a gas bomb tossed into a hotel room. Bullets fired into the home of a county field representative of the union killed his teen-age son. Such tactics to break the union occurred in a county whose local government was notoriously corrupt and antiunion. In three years time, Sheriff Middleton accumulated $92,000 on a salary of $5,000 a year and emerged from the strife as a major mine owner.

The miners could count on little help from outside the county. Kentucky's state government sent troops to restore order, but did nothing to end corruption in the county government. The National Recovery Administration established fair standards for the coal industry, which the companies systematically ignored. Of 708 complaints of violations of NRA filed with the Bituminous Coal Labor Board, 90 came from Harlan County.

Violations of basic constitutional rights became so well known that in 1937 the LaFollette Civil Liberties Committee visited the county to investigate. Earlier reports by prominent labor sympathizers such as Theodore Dreiser, John Dos Passos, and Sherwood Anderson had done little good. The LaFollette committee, however, documented a sordid landscape of operator dominance of the county power structure, of a system of private deputy sheriffs employed by the mines, and of violations of civil liberties. With national opinion spotlighting Bloody Harlan, the system by which mines employed county deputy sheriffs was abolished, destroying the chief instrument of antiunionism. By April 1937, the UMW had reentered the county. With its organizers under federal protection, UMW membership climbed from 1,200 in 1935 to 9,000 by September 1937. The operators finally signed a union contract that referred disputes to collective bargaining. Arbitration and negotiation replaced violence, and not a single life was lost because of labor-management disputes during the ensuing two decades. Federal New Deal activity in the county also created a new balance of political power in Harlan, with the UMW emerging as the major factor and the county switching from predominantly Republican to solidly Democratic. In the coal region, Franklin D. Roosevelt was venerated as highly as UMW President John L. Lewis.

The collapse of the Communist NMWU was similar to the failure of so many government programs later designed to assist the poor people of Appalachia. It failed not so much because of its inability to educate miners about the class struggle; no one understood exploitation better than a desperate Kentucky coal miner. Rather, the Communists neither comprehended nor appreciated the unique character and culture of these people. They did not effectively counter or utilize the individualism, fatalism, or religious beliefs of mountain people. Leftist organizers and miners might struggle alongside each other on the picket line for common goals, but they belonged culturally to different worlds.

Perhaps the ultimate irony for workers followed in the wake of labor's victory in Harlan County. Labor contracts so improved wages that the mines began to mechanize, and a process which had begun years earlier raced ahead in the 1940s and 1950s. Technology proved a more formidable adversary than the company-owned sheriffs of Harlan County. It took only 140,000 miners in 1964 to produce more coal than 700,000 had torn from the mountains in 1914. The loss of mining jobs between 1950 and 1959 alone was 265,000. Devices for boring directly into the coal seam eliminated undercutting and blasting. Conveyor belts replaced tracks and coal cars. Roof bolting was both safer and more economical than using timber for support. A single mechanical loading machine could load more coal than two dozen men with shovels. Small mines were purchased by larger corporations and mechanized. By the 1950s three out of every four eastern Kentucky miners were idled, and the welfare philosophy of the federal government was no more able to assist unemployed industrial workers living in a rural environment than it had been in 1929.

Appalachian Dislocation/Migration

Mechanization brought another catastrophe to the mountains in the 1950s when small commercial farms on the edges of the hills could no longer compete with mechanized units to the east and south. Between 1950 and 1959 the number of commercial farms in Appalachia declined by 38.8 percent. The total loss of jobs in mining and farming within the region in the decade of the 1950s amounted to 600,000. Regional economic growth in other industries absorbed only about half of these.

Unemployed Appalachians could leave (a third of them did), or they could retreat up the hollows and go on welfare. If they stayed in Appalachia, they were dominated by local political machines, which controlled school boards and county jobs, critical sources of employment that constituted the largest payrolls.

The other option, migration out of Appalachia, was no more attractive. Although out-migration has been most apparent during the past quarter century, it had long been a method by which mountain people sought better lives. By the 1840s the southern Appalachians had become overcrowded. Some emigrants, seeking land similar to what they were leaving, crossed the Mississippi River and traveled west to the Ozark-Ouachita Mountains of Arkansas and southern Missouri. Others crossed the prairies in the nineteenth century and settled in the Cascades, along the coastal ranges of Washington and Oregon, or scattered amid the valleys of the northern Rockies.

The Texas hill country in the central portion of the Lone Star State attracted its share of mountain folk. Obviously these people passed through better land, notably the Blackland Prairie, in order to reach mountainous terrain that was inferior in soil quality. In these remote regions, Appalachian culture could be kept intact despite the geographic breach. Appalachian descriptive names such as "gap," "cove," and "hollow" survived into the modern era. Some seventeen major family feuds occurred in the Texas hill country before 1900. Economically this region was also the poorest in Texas; of 21 hill counties, 17 had median family incomes below 4,000 dollars in 1960.

Even in the Cascades and the Wilapa Hills far to the west Appalachian culture persisted. Mountain ways of forest exploitation, subsistence agriculture, and folklore survived decades of separation from the nourishment of the Highlands. Appalachian dialect, music, handicrafts, religion, and politics endured.

Unfortunately, the surplus population of depression days had no mountains left to pioneer. Their escape valve was the city, and a new and equally insidious exploitation was too often their fate. Despite a decline in the 1960s, Appalachia maintained the highest birth rate of any American region during the twentieth century. Opposition to birth control abated among town people and in the more prosperous valleys, but remained strong among the poorest and most isolated whites.

The post-World War II new immigrant from the South was mainly young, poorly educated, and white. Although such people were lumped together in the negative category "hillbilly," less than half of the rural Southern whites who entered Northern cities were from the mountains. Sociologist Rupert Vance had suggested in 1944 that such migration to areas offering better economic opportunities provided the most promising solution to the plight of the mountain population. Between 1940 and 1970 more than two million people took his advice, leaving the southern Highlands for industrial cities. Since the mountaineer was an internal immigrant, it was assumed that he had no adjustment to make. Once again, his distinctive culture proved his undoing.

The clash in values between past experience and the new urban setting was devastating. Back home they had valued a community level of existence; they did not wish to be thought different from or better than their neighbors. They accepted their integral place in the community without the need to compete for status. Their identity and value to the community were determined by birth, sex, and age. In the new urban environment, great value was placed upon achieving, upon rising above their neighbor's status. Kinship lost its significance. In short, mountain people found that their status and identity depended upon behavior that they had not been taught to value.

Confused and leaderless, these migrants faced a tremendously complex structure of public services, which they needed in order to survive. The social institution that demonstrated greatest interest in their welfare was the church. But the groups that most frequently offered assistance were Catholic, Lutheran, and Methodist churches very different from the Pentecostal and fundamentalist sects of their homes. These established denominations conducted more liturgical services, which were stiff and formal and not wholly satisfying. Few mountain people attended a local church regularly, and when they did, it was likely to be a storefront Pentecostal church. Yet, nearly all mountain migrants regarded themselves as religious and considered faith the most important factor in curing diseases. The success of churches such as

Rex Humbard's Cathedral of Tomorrow and Ernest Angley's Grace Cathedral in Akron demonstrated the persistence of Appalachian religious beliefs.

The tenacity with which mountain people clung to their beliefs despite pressure to conform can be seen in every sphere of their lives. Urban blacks proved the efficacy of community organization in obtaining assistance. Despite this example, mountain whites who came to the city retained their traditional independence from all organizations, and as a result they were ignored by government programs designed for the poor.

Accessibility to medical care furnished an excellent example of the persistence of traditional culture despite demonstrated need. Detroit, Michigan, contained an estimated 30,000 Southern white immigrants in 1970, and made prenatal medical care available on the basis of ability to pay; but Southern mountain women did not seek the help. This refusal to obtain assistance resulted from a conflict between traditional mountain values and the attitudes of medically educated urban professionals. Poor women from the Southern mountains distrusted physicians; traditionally modest, they were humiliated by prenatal and postnatal examinations. They also retained great respect for traditional folk medicine and remedies.

The traditional role of women also interfered with adequate medical treatment in other ways. In the mountains, women had been the primary transmitters of medical lore, and they determined when to summon physicians. In the city, they could not fulfill their traditional role. The herbs and roots necessary to remedies were not available, and the mountain women had to substitute patent medicines. Also, in the mountains "her man" had been responsible for contacting the doctor and providing transportation. Women were supposed to stay at home and be seen in public as little as possible. In Detroit the man was at work, and the woman had to master the intricacies of public transportation in order to get to a free clinic. Usually, mountain women delayed going to the doctor until a crisis arose, then had to use slow public transport, only to be confronted by the mountainous pile of red tape at a welfare medical center. Public health personnel sometimes added to the problem by discourteous and demeaning conduct; mountain people, always sensitive to hillbilly stereotyping, frequently found offense where none was intended.

The clash between mountain people and physicians was not entirely a product of displacement. The conflicting cultural assumptions that underlay such problems continued to exist in the mountains. Relationships among mountain folk were personal. Acceptance depended on kinship, on whether a person was local, a recognized member of the community; negative status came from being an unknown outsider. Yet, many medical professionals related to people impersonally and objectively. To be treated as an object was a dehumanizing insult to mountain people, while it was accepted as a necessary inconvenience among urban folk.

Oftentimes the migrant from Appalachia considered himself only a temporary resident of the city. When initial aspirations for a better life were frustrated, he became bitter, tended to glorify the past he left behind in the hills, and took refuge in mountain attitudes and values. The tenacity of past beliefs and practices made conflict with urban values more intense.

The life of Jim Hammitte illustrated the plight of an uprooted poor mountaineer. Born in southeastern Kentucky in 1916, he was the oldest of thirteen children and the son of an illiterate coal miner. He quit school at the age of fifteen and entered the mines the next year in 1932. In 1942 he left Harlan County, Kentucky, for a war plant in Detroit where he worked until he retired to the hill country of north Alabama in the 1960s. His problems in Detroit, his perceptions of life there, echoed the experience of thousands:

Q. The neighborhood you lived in, were there a lot of people there who came from the South?

A. There were a lot of people there came from the South but it was hard to get acquainted with them because once you moved into the city the friendly atmosphere that we were used to no longer exists. You pass people on the street, they don't talk to you—you don't talk to them. If you tried to smile and talk to somebody, why they thought you's up to something, gonna rob them or something so, and this was another thing that bothered you real bad, you go into a store to shop, there's nobody you could talk to, nobody. You walk up to the corner like you normally do, you could not talk to people. . . .

. . . .

Q. Was there a lot of discrimination against the Southerners, like at your job, having to do with promotions?

A. Yes, they was a lot of discrimination on the job or in the city. As far as promotions, I can't say that. But you had a constant be on your toes, have your guard up for Southern language you used because if you spilled some of it out and it wasn't according to hoyle, why some Northern person grab it and poke fun at you immediately and the ones that could cope with it and roll and joke back come through all right. The ones that took issue with it had a terrible time. And as far as I'm concerned, the North was as much or more critical of Southern people than Southern people has ever been of Northern people. And to my opinion this still exists.

. . . .

Q. How much did you keep in touch with the people back home?

A. Well, I was the oldest one of 13 and my father got killed in the coal mine when I was 21 so I more or less took the responsibility of the father. So I kept close touch with the family and as each one got older I helped them prepare and found them a job, helped them get started. So, as they got older, I'd bring them from home up there, help them get started in the plants, or a job, so I was in constant contact with the people back home. And her mother and father was here, too, so we kept close contact. This seemed to be one of the worst things of Southern people going north. We're so close in our relation with each other, it was just hard to separate yourself from the family and going north was one of the worse difficulties you can imagine. Pulling yourself away from the family, you know, church on Sundays, Sunday dinner at one of the houses, and visit 2 or 3 times a week, or doing it all the time. I lived in a mining community where I could see my grandmother daily, half dozen uncles, aunts and when you move out away from that moving to a strange city, it was really hard to adjust to.

. . . .

Q. How many children do you have?

A. We have 3 kids.

Q. Did you all have hospitalization or a doctor when they were born?

A. We had one doctor. We lived in the coal mining field when the two was born, the boy and the girl. We had a company doctor that lived in the community. We were 18 miles from town where the hospital was. But them days you never bothered to go to the hospital for a baby to be born. They either had a midwife, they call them, or the doctor, though in our case the doctor come to the house and a couple of neighbor ladies, friends come in to help and that's the way babies was born. And come time for the third baby to be born, she wasn't about to go to the hospital in Detroit. She insisted on coming home to her mother and that's where the baby was born by another company doctor coming in the house.[2]

Stereotypes about mountain culture crippled poor white mountain people as badly as similar generalizations hurt blacks. The cognitive word to which all other terms were related was "hillbilly." The word evoked the same emotions among mountain whites that "nigger" did among blacks. Friends might use it when talking to each other, but the term was taboo for outsiders. Many urban Americans believed that hillbillies were antisocial, suspicious, lazy, poor tenants, placed low value on education, clannish, disease-ridden, drank too much, belonged to Holiness, faith-healing churches when they attended at all, and were prone to incest and statutory rape. A magazine as respected as *Harper's* featured an article entitled "The Hillbillies Invade Chicago" in February 1958, which contained all these stereotypes.

Attempts to open communications and dissolve some of these attitudes began in the 1950s. The Council of the Southern Mountains sponsored a series of workshops at Berea College in Kentucky, which brought together social workers and educators from Chicago, Detroit, Cleveland, and Cincinnati. There, mountain culture was explained to them. From these yearly seminars came Chicago's special remedial classes for mountain children. The Chicago Boys Club began to sponsor special projects for migrant boys from Appalachia. Cincinnati created committees to help eliminate job discrimination. Other cities tried to develop leadership among mountain whites. Such projects reflected comprehension that regional subculture could isolate poor people from the mainstream as fully as race.

Discovering Appalachian Poverty

By the 1960s, out-migration had made Southern poverty a national issue, and Appalachia was the most frequently cited example. Long obscured in their remote mountain redoubts, Appalachia's poor were featured in articles that appeared in *Look, Life, U. S. News and World Report, The Nation,* and *The New York Times Magazine.* Academic journals and presidential commissions documented the wretched condition of mountain people.

Federal agencies defined the southern Appalachians as an area consisting of 80,000 square miles occupying parts of nine states and containing eight million people. In 1949 more than sixty percent of the people in two-thirds of the mountain counties from West Virginia to Alabama had cash incomes of less than $2,000. Full-time farmers in the same area averaged a net income of less than $500 annually. Three-fourths of the people were rural in 1960, and the median family income was no higher than in 1949—still about $2,000 a year or less than half the national average. Between 1950 and 1970, 69 percent of the region's coal mine work force was displaced, reducing the number of miners from 475,245 in 1950 to 198,839 in 1960. The states most directly affected, especially Kentucky and West Virginia, were disaster areas. By 1959 some 600,000 Kentuckians or 20 percent of the state's population had established eligibility for relief from the federal surplus food distribution program.

Entire Appalachian counties were hopelessly mired in poverty. In Martin County, Kentucky, half the population was on public assistance. The only local industry consisted of several small sawmills. Extreme poverty, poor education, inadequate diet, third-generation welfare cases, and out-migration of the young were characteristic. Leslie

County, Kentucky, lost more than 25 percent of its population between 1952 and 1959, most of it to Cincinnati, Columbus, Detroit, and South Bend.

In 1965 *The New York Times Magazine* printed Reese Cleghorn's probing biography of Dawson County, Georgia, the smallest of the state's thirty-five Appalachian counties. The all white population of 3,590 earned a per capita annual income of only $1,209; 58 percent of the *employed* males earned *less* than $2,000 per year, and only 16 percent earned more than $4,000. Among residents twenty-five years or older, 63 percent had not completed the eighth-grade, and only 15 percent had finished high school. Despite its beautiful scenery and mineral resources, the county's population had declined rapidly (it had more people in 1859 than in 1960), and it did not contain a single doctor, dentist, or lawyer. Eighty percent of the county's students ate free lunches provided by the federal school lunch program, although some insisted on doing work in return for the meals. The only industry was a low-wage shirt factory.

Renewed public interest allowed President Kennedy to appoint the Appalachian Regional Commission. Consisting of representatives designated by the governor of each Appalachian state and from all major federal departments and agencies, its task was to propose a unified strategy to develop the region. It designated 340 Appalachian counties with a mostly white population of more than fifteen million as its target area. The commission's report graphically depicted economic inequities: one of every three families lived on an annual income of less than $3,000; unemployment in 1960 was 7.1 percent compared to 5 percent in the rest of the country; new employment in the decade of the 1950s had increased only 1.5 percent compared to a 15 percent rise elsewhere in the country. Of those over twenty-five years of age, only 32 of every 100 had finished high school, contrasted to almost 42 of every 100 elsewhere.

Commission recommendations dealt with human as well as economic resources, with the largest sum devoted to highway construction. Its five-year proposal carried a price tag of 4.5 billion dollars, with Washington funding three billion. In 1965 Congress passed a scaled-down Appalachian Development Act authorizing the expenditure of 840 million dollars for highways over a six-year period, with an additional 252 million dollars for other projects to be spent over a two-year span. In 1967, Congress increased the highway authorization to a little more than 1 billion dollars, but provided only 170 million dollars more for nonhighway projects during a second two-year period. John L. Sweeney, federal cochairman of the Appalachian Regional Commission created by the 1965 Act, argued a rather obvious conclusion of the Congress: building 3,350 miles of highway would remove the greatest barrier to Appalachian development, its geographical isolation. By spending money where there was maximum growth potential and ignoring remote areas, the Commission would encourage industry to locate near existing urban areas and hopefully persuade the remote poor to move nearer them.

No doubt there were sound economic reasons for the designation of four-fifths of these monies to highway construction. Also, political pragmatism dictated this priority since the governors and congressmen who represented the region desired that road construction be given priority. Provision of health facilities, vocational education, reclamation of mining areas, and development of timber resources received inadequate funding when the scaled-down program passed Congress. Like most of the poverty programs of the 1960s, this Act attempted to increase the economic opportunities open to the poor without threatening major institutions or vested interests. This assured its passage but hindered its accomplishments.

Although the regional approach to economic development had considerable political appeal, its impact on the poor was less certain. Most obviously, it was a long-term approach that might require a generation to substantially improve conditions. Also, it gambled heavily that new highways and factories would resolve complex problems. Its administration was enmeshed in state and regional petty politics. At the same time that economist John Friedmann suggested that any successful program must obtain the support of Appalachian people themselves, he envisioned an urbanized and altered region, which could not hope to appeal to many of those people: "The metropolitan centers of Appalachia must shed their dreary 19th-century facades, exchange blue-collar for white-collar jobs, and reject provincialism in favor of a more cosmopolitan outlook." Appalachian culture, born and sustained by its isolation, was now expected to welcome interstates, industrialism, urbanism, and modernity.

The Appalachian Development Program was too conservative and was designed to pass Congress by avoiding any real challenge to "conventional economic wisdom." Although highways helped, jobs constituted the critical need, and the development program created relatively few. Automated industry would not relocate in remote mountains just to obtain cheap labor. The congressional appropriation could have been spent more wisely on improved housing, creation of better schools and health facilities, reforestation, stream cleanup, and reclamation of strip-mined land. As an article in *The Nation* concluded, the congressional program was "only a modest down payment—a feeble step toward the kind of comprehensive regional development programs that the nation needs."

Successes and Failures

Because Appalachia attracted primary regional attention in the 1960s, progress there may serve as a gauge to the success of poverty programs. No less than five major congressional enactments affected the Southern mountains: the Area Redevelopment Act of 1961, the Public Works Acceleration Act of 1962, the Public Works and Economic Development Act of 1965, the Appalachian Redevelopment Act of 1962, and the Economic Opportunity Act of 1965. Despite some progress occasioned by this activity, Appalachia continued to play its historic role as a barrier to east-west commerce and still generated economic activity in the 1970s at a slower rate than the rest of the nation.

The multistate region encompassed by the Appalachian Regional Commission actually contained many Appalachias, which registered markedly different growth patterns during the 1960s. Some mountain counties in the Carolinas, Tennessee, and Alabama experienced rapid growth; others in Kentucky, Virginia, and West Virginia lagged behind national growth rates.

The Appalachian economy was more closely linked with economic activities outside the region than with those within, West Virginia serving as the best example. Three factors inhibited the state's economic growth: nonstandard transportation, paucity of public investment due to state governmental attitudes, and the industrial structure of the state.

Transportation is critical in a market-directed economy. Cost of distribution is the dominant factor in plant location for many industries. West Virginia's poor road system inhibited industries that depended on truck transportation either for obtaining raw materials or for distribution. The Appalachian highway system of some 2,500 miles contained a high percentage of steep, narrow, winding roads, which restricted trucks and consequently slowed industrial growth. In 1971 before highway speeds were lowered, the average auto travel speed in West Virginia was only 45 miles per hour while the average for trucks was well below that. Low-wage industry, which might have located in labor-rich West Virginia, avoided the state because such industry relied on cheap truck transportation.

Governmental structure, public investment, and regional attitudes compounded the transportation problem. West Virginia has experienced trouble raising the ten percent matching funds required by the federal interstate highway program, and the Appalachian Regional Commission required an even larger share of state funding. The rural-dominated state legislature had siphoned a disproportionate share of state highway funds into building and maintaining country roads. Furthermore, taxing and spending policies were controlled by the same body. The state relied heavily on a regressive general sales tax for revenue instead of a tax on income produced, which would have broadened the tax base.

West Virginia's major resource was coal, and the crisis in international petroleum economics sparked a reappraisal of coal as a basic energy source despite ecological objections to strip mining. Pike County, Kentucky, which possessed the most extensive underground coal production in America, increased employment from 4,500 in 1964 to 8,000 in 1968. The industry expanded even more in the 1970s. Basing any long-term solution to Appalachian woes on the resurgence of the coal industry, however, was a risky strategy. The utilization of atomic and solar energy by the Tennessee Valley Authority and private power companies might damn Appalachia to yet another cycle of technological unemployment.

The growth of diversified small industries and tourism offered a more permanent solution. Some progress was made in both these areas. Federal and state parks scattered throughout the region opened some of America's most spectacular scenery to vacationers, and the people's conservation mood heightened interest in wilderness areas. The renewal of interest in folk culture also popularized isolated regions. As Florida discovered long ago, tourists served the local economy quite as well as factories, and no area of America possessed greater natural assets than Appalachia.

Mainstream Values and Subcultural Persistence

Understanding Appalachian culture became a critical challenge to those trying to design economic programs to help alleviate poverty. The principal elements of mountain subculture were individualism and self-reliance, traditionalism and fatalism, familism, and religious fundamentalism.

Individualism was perhaps the most historic characteristic of Appalachian poor whites; it brought them to the solitude of the mountains and kept them there for generations. Isolated externally from the mainstream and internally from each other, they learned to make what they needed to survive, or to do without. Midwives birthed their children, and mountain artisans developed remarkable skills of craftsmanship. They resented authority, whether the source was royal governors before the Revolution or centralized state agencies later. They shirked responsibilities to the larger community and avoided civic and social involvements.

Individualism also governed the interpersonal relationships of mountain people. They seldom reacted neutrally, and they expected to be treated as persons, not as objects. Their church life encompassed an individualistic egalitarianism. In the Primitive Baptist Church, requirements for leadership were simple: one must be "called" by the Lord. Neither education nor theological training could enhance one's qualifications. When missionaries from well-organized coastal churches reached the mountains, more often than not they encountered a hostile reception. Appalachian Christians maintained their separation from Southern Baptist and Methodist denominational authority, and their churches remained the most independent in American Christendom.

No aspect of mountain culture ran more counter to the mainstream of American values than fatalism. Most Americans were achievement oriented, and few ideas had such universal support in the nation's past as the work ethic. Countless government programs established in the twentieth century to bring economic changes to the mountains failed because of the absence of a work ethic among the people. The willingness of the mountain people to reconcile themselves to deprivation and to passively accept it as fate and "God's will" was both frustrating and inscrutable to the bureaucrats who administered government programs. The fatalism of the mountain people, born of a long and arduous association with their environment, seemed to their would-be helpers as nothing more than shiftlessness and laziness.

Most Americans could not comprehend a subculture that accepted life as it was, that "made do with what the Good Lord provided." In the mountains, time was more related to seasons and the rhythm of generations than to clocks. There was more time to study the plants and wildflowers in the springtime, to lay off work in order to go hunting or fishing, to rock on the porch, or to visit with friends. Why should one strive when such effort never seemed to do any good, where planning was difficult, where getting ahead appeared to be impossible?

When asked, "Do you think that God is more pleased when people are satisfied with what they have or when they try to get ahead?" three-fourths of the Appalachian poor replied that God was pleased when people were satisfied. Such a notion fitted a world where all hopes for the future were contingent. A slate fall, a tornado, too much rain or

not enough, and all aspirations came to nothing. A ballad entitled
"Rye Cove" told of a cyclone that blew a mountain schoolhouse away,
taking the lives of thirteen children. It reminded mountain people how
tentative and ephemeral life was.

> Oh, listen today at a story I'll tell,
> Of a sadness and tear-dimmed eye;
> Of a dreadful cyclone that came this May,
> And blew our schoolhouse away.
>
> *Chorus*
> Rye Cove
> Rye Cove
>
> The place of my childhood and home;
> Where life's early morn,
> I once loved to roam,
> But now it's so silent and lone.
>
> When the cyclone appeared it darkened the air,
> The lightning flashed over the sky;
> And the children all cried,
> Don't take us away, but spare us to go back home.
>
> *Chorus*
>
> There were mothers so dear,
> And fathers the same;
> That came to that horrible scene,
> Searching and crying—each found its own child;
> Dying on a pillow of stone.
>
> *Chorus*
>
> Oh, give me a home,
> Far beyond the blue sky;
> Where the storms and cyclones are unknown,
> And there will I stand—will clasp the glad hand;
> Our children in their heavenly home.
>
> *Chorus*

The fatalism of mountain culture, so often criticized by outsiders, served as a sane and functional protective device. Where life was harsh and little was expected, failure was accepted more easily; people were satisfied just to "get by." Fatalism was a realistic appraisal of life experiences. Mountain poor people were powerless, they recognized this fact, and they learned to cope with it. They made the best of their lives, lived from day to day, and drew comfort and pleasure from kinfolk, from the beauty of the seasons, from hunting and fishing, from the expectation that someday they would abide in "a beautiful home by the bright crystal sea . . . where no one will be a stranger to me."

Familism assumed that an individual's obligations to his kin held priority over duties to other individuals or groups. Mountain people often subordinated personal desires to family duties. One's value depended heavily on "who you are"; that is, who your father was and where he came from. Just as kinship determined loyalties, it determined animosities, as in the legendary mountain feuds.

Some outsiders have blamed religion for fatalism and other harmful aspects of Appalachian culture. Mountain people did view God from their own angle; but in this they were no different from other Christians. The same God who could be comprehended by a literal reading of scripture, who created man without the necessity of evolution, that same deity governed the seasons and the course of history, cared for them in a personal way, knew their names and numbered the hairs of their heads. If they were "yesterday's people," they were also God's people, uniquely possessing His revelation and living true to it.

Psychiatrist Robert Coles lived among the mountain people whom he described in a Pulitzer Prize-winning trilogy. He respected their faith and denied that the religion was wholly escapist. In fact, their religion was essential to their notions of self-worth and helped them make sense out of their lives.

Many students of southern Appalachia reached a less flattering conclusion when they attempted to relate folk character to the contemporary problems of the mountains. Following a detailed analysis of white poverty in the hills, two sociologists concluded in 1970 that the "socialization system" of mountain families and schools suppressed the "pro-social aggressive techniques that are necessary for the lower strata to take part in the more normal distribution of resources." They proposed that mountain men must change their ways. The "stubbornness" and "passive aggression" of Appalachian people must give way to the realization that reward came from "struggling positively against the system." Such advice ran counter to the history and culture of three hundred years. It is no wonder that the mountains became a graveyard for the ideals of social workers who entered the hills determined to change the character of a people as the initial step in their secular redemption.

Another recent sociological analysis of Appalachia reached an equally questionable conclusion. Prolonged frustration had "institutionalized nonrational response," creating an "analgesic subculture." This jargon sought to explain why mountain people resigned themselves to welfare, refused to leave the mountains for better opportunities elsewhere, and lacked ambition. Generations of misfortune caused young people to anticipate defeat; from this anticipation they developed a subculture to lessen its impact upon them. When sustained over a long period of time, the study concluded, the result was a relapse into barbarism, which could be seen in the lack of aesthetics, anti-intellectualism, literalism in interpreting the Bible, superstition, and reliance on welfare. Yet, this same subculture produced handicrafts of great skill and beauty. The eloquent eulogy of an ancient mountain man explaining at a "homecoming" that he will not meet his friends again "this side the vale," may be based on Biblical literalism, but it is also a meaningful statement of one person's view of ultimate reality. The fatalism of the "analgesic subculture" seemed more a logical explanation than a contrived analgesic; if an analgesic, it was more rational than irrational.

Some sociologists created an obstacle to the understanding of Appalachian culture by insisting that the region's economic poverty was closely related to a culture of poverty. The culture of poverty model unfavorably compared the subculture of the southern Appalachians to dominant American values. Most sociological studies of the mountains have emphasized these "quaint differences" and found them to be disorganizing, defeating, and obsolete. Traditionalism, fatalism, laziness, and apathy all were blamed. But none of these models explain why such indigence prevailed.

Recently, sociologist Helen Lewis has challenged this model and offered in its place a subculture forged in economic exploitation. Appalachian poor people were alienated and deprived through the operation of a specific economic and political system. Those who controlled the resources preserved their advantage by discrimination against the poor. Mountain people were not essentially passive and fatalistic; these attitudes were merely adjustive techniques of powerless people, ways by which they protected themselves from outside culture.

Obviously, not all mountain white poverty can be blamed on economic colonialism any more than it can be attributed entirely to the personal failure of Appalachia poor whites; but this new model does provide a useful corrective.

When coal mines, textile mills, and lumber companies invaded Appalachia in the last years of the nineteenth century, they encountered a society not unlike that of Asia and Africa in economic foundations. Speculators purchased land, mineral, and timber rights from illiterate, subsistence farmers. The transfer of titles and land in eastern Kentucky contained many cases of fraudulent leases. A survival of this practice was the Broad Form deed, which has been upheld by Kentucky courts. Such deeds covered "all minerals and metallic substances and all combination of the same," which can be removed by any method "deemed necessary or convenient." Uninformed mountain people transferred their mineral rights, then years later watched helplessly while their land was strip-mined. In a recent widely celebrated case, "Widow" Combs stopped bulldozers by lying down in front of them and ended up in the Knott County jail.

One evidence of the extent of colonial control emerged from the patterns of land and mineral ownership in the mountains. Tax records and Bureau of Mines documents in the eleven leading coal-producing counties in eastern Kentucky revealed that thirty-one people and corporations owned four-fifths of the region's coal. Four or five large corporations owned seventy to eighty percent of the minerals found in southwest Virginia. In 1969, seven firms produced one-third of the total coal mined in central Appalachia (Kentucky, West Virginia, western Virginia).

Furthermore, many ostensibly independent companies were linked together in corporate structures. There was a close connection between railroad owners, industrialists, and financiers who owned and benefited from the timber and mineral wealth of the region. Some of the interlocking corporate relationships extended beyond the American border and involved diversified industries such as electronics, petrochemicals, banks, and automobile manufacturers.

These companies made exceptional profits. According to its 1968 Annual Report, the Penn Virginia Corporation netted sixty-four percent on its gross investment and paid dividends of forty cents out of each dollar received. Such profits were characteristic of mining companies operating in the region. In addition, state and federal governments favored companies with depletion and depreciation allowances and advantageous tax structures. In the early 1970s, Virginia taxes on mining machinery amounted to one-tenth its value, compared to a tax rate of one-third value for other businesses. In 1971 West Virginia had a gross sales tax, but coal companies did not pay a tax on most of their sales because they were made out of state. In earlier years the mines were even more blatantly exploitive. Company doctors refused to admit the existence of pneumoconiosis (black lung), workers who joined the UMW were expelled from company houses and were given the hardest jobs underground, and local politicians and law enforcement officials often ignored violence directed against labor organizers.

The more blatant aspects of economic colonialism have disappeared in Appalachia; revelation of another feudal company fiefdom—such as Harlan County, Kentucky, in the 1930s—is unlikely. Yet, the vestiges of colonialism remained. In 1971 Joseph Routh, board chairman of Pittston Corporation, donated $350,000 to Cornell University in Ithaca, New York, to provide artificial turf for the university football field. Pittston Corporation held major interests in coal, trucking, and oil distribution within Appalachia. Cheap labor and the exploitation of mineral and labor resources explained part of the corporation's success. Earl Malizia wrote sardonically in *Appalachian Journal* that perhaps Cornell's letter of appreciation for the artificial turf should have been sent to the coal miners and truckers employed by Pittston.

Nor were labor unions without responsibility for the enduring problems of Appalachia. The UMW came to dominate the lives of many Harlan County miners after 1937. It became increasingly corrupt, and by the 1960s there were allegations that UMW officials took kickbacks from mine owners to accept "sweetheart contracts," which were favorable to the companies. Older miners interested mainly in pensions elected William Turnblazer president of the Harlan UMW local, and Turnblazer, in turn, supported UMW president Tony Boyle. When insurgent reform leader Jock Yablonski ran against Boyle, he refused to campaign in Harlan because of threats to his life. In a highly publicized trial in 1970, Turnblazer and three other area miners were convicted of murdering Yablonski and his family, and Boyle was subsequently convicted also.

Although economics was the clearest example of colonialism, culture did not escape either. Missionaries and educators often functioned as legitimizers of exploitation. Without realizing it, they subtly taught mountain folk that their ways were backward, even barbaric. Many of the outlanders who entered the mountains in the late nineteenth century were women because females were more readily accepted. One such missionary was Alice Lloyd, who came from Boston to Troublesome Creek in Kentucky to help the poor people of Appalachia. A local mountain man gave her one hundred fifty acres for a school so she could teach his children to live "not liken to the hog but unliken the hog." Another missionary drove a wagon into Hazard, Kentucky, in 1895:

> Folks couldn't rightly make out why she had come all that weary way up into Perry County; she had no people here that anyone could see. . . . She was friendly, "nice-spoken," "a little bit nosey," "visited nearly every family," "stayed the night," "would pitch in and help," and sometimes she'd come right out and rail at them over doing something a wrong way or a hard way and show them a *better way*. Miss Pettit had such a way about her that she got by with it.[3]

Sincere, dedicated missionaries profoundly affected mountaineers. Families moved closer to settlements so their children could attend schools. The missionaries and teachers provided skills and trained leaders, improved health and social services. But they sometimes made mountain people ashamed of their culture. The fasola music of Primitive Baptists was too brittle and disharmonious; mountain life too independent and undisciplined. Traditional ballads and instruments were too "country" and were replaced in one community by operettas such as the "Windmill of Holland" and "Quest of the Pink Parasol." Churches and schools taught the values of organization and planning. Such denial of traditions by institutions that mountain children respected made many of them ashamed of their heritage. Teachers and missionaries helped legitimize economic exploitation by blaming Appalachian ills entirely on the mountaineer and his ways. Few of them recognized that the economic system shared the blame. Even those who appreciated mountain crafts and music or the simple, genuine worship of Appalachian religious sects considered lack of organization and education, and irregular worship services to be serious problems.

Such attitudes resulted in a defensive reaction by mountain people. Preachers from the hills insisted that the indwelling spirit of God meant more than theological training. They favorably contrasted the individualism of Primitive Baptists to the cooperative hierarchy created by Methodists and Missionary Baptists. They preferred informality and freedom to express emotions to stiffer and more liturgical forms of worship.

Although Southern Baptists and Methodists attracted converts in the mountains in the nineteenth century, their primary strength was in the towns and among Appalachian people who moved into the middle class. Many unchurched folk became Free Will Baptists, Pentecostals, or joined one of the more obscure sects.

The snake-handling cult of the twentieth century was the most unusual to originate in the mountains. During the summer of 1909, George Went Hensley, a Pentecostal preacher, initiated the rite of snake-handling in the remote hamlet of Sale Creek in southeastern

Tennessee. He based the practice on a literal reading of verses seventeen and eighteen in the sixteenth chapter of Mark: "And these signs shall follow them that believe; In my name shall they cast out devils; they shall speak with new tongues; They shall take up serpents; and if they drink any deadly thing, it shall not hurt them; they shall lay hands on the sick, and they shall recover." Most holiness congregations rejected the practice, but not all of them. Hensley allegedly was bitten four hundred times over forty-five years of handling deadly rattlesnakes and copperheads before he was fatally bitten in a service near Altha, Florida, on July 24, 1955. He was one of at least thirty-five fatalities that occurred between 1936 and 1973. Strychnine poisoning accounted for at least five additional deaths. Despite these fatalities, the churches spread. By the 1970s there were snake-handling churches in Kentucky, Tennessee, Alabama, Georgia, the Carolinas, Florida, West Virginia, Virginia, Ohio, Indiana, and Michigan. Most states forbade the practice following the snakebite deaths of two West Virginia female handlers in 1961, but the cult simply went underground.

The services usually occurred on Saturday and Sunday nights. They included both sexes and all ages who met in a simple rectangular frame church building or one constructed of concrete blocks. Their musical instruments were traditional mountain instruments, especially the guitar; these were accompanied by rhythmic clapping and foot stomping. The preacher was a fellow laborer who seldom received a salary. Services were emotional with much physical activity: shouting, crying, dancing, trembling, swaying, whirling about, jumping up and down, and falling to the floor. As the excitement mounted, snakes were taken from their containers, and the "handling" lasted for about an hour and a half. If bitten, the snake-handlers usually rejected medical assistance. One Tennessee handler explained:

> I've been bitten twice, but I didn't go to no doctor. I let the best doctor there is—Doctor Jesus—take care of me. Them medical doctors start hacking you up . . . why, you're more likely to die if you go to them than if you put your trust in Jesus. A lot of people in this church have been bitten, but not a one has lost a finger, a hand, or life.[4]

Snake-handlers were mostly coal miners, factory workers, and sub-sistence farmers of Scotch-Irish and English origin. Their cosmology was based upon a literal reading of the Bible, their sermons empha-sized the vicarious death of Jesus, His imminent second coming, judg-ment and everlasting life, miraculous signs and wonders. They were otherworldly and ascetic, rejecting the existing social order as corrupt and beyond redemption. Their most important objective was to ob-tain spiritual gifts, which were manifested by their ability to speak in unknown tongues, prophesy, work miracles, heal the sick, cast out devils, handle snakes, or drink poison.

The cult was an enigma, a classic confrontation between cultures. Snake-handling occurred most frequently not in the most isolated re-gions of Appalachia, but in peripheral areas undergoing change from subsistence agriculture to industry. The cult helped its members cope with the humiliation attendant to being poor and a hillbilly. One way to adjust to threatening new values was to reject them, and the snake-handling group demonstrated the tension of people torn from decades of isolation and thrust into the modern world.

Ironically, the tension among snake-handlers and Pentecostals was both toward the present and past, toward industrial values and the traditional ways of the mountains. They suppressed older Appalachian traditions in favor of exclusive loyalty to the sect. They opposed both traditional and modern dance forms, yet snake-handlers incorporated in worship a rhythmic hop and skip. They rejected folk remedies, yet retained a suspicion of doctors common to generations of mountain people. Smoking, drinking, moonshining, folksongs, telling tall tales, and feuding were all taboo. Despite opposition to such traditional prac-tices, converts were not asked to substitute secular urban values in place of traditional ones. Instead, they retreated into an individualistic sectarianism that isolated them as completely from twentieth-century values as their remote hollows had cut them off geographically. To people who were yanked into the modern world by the need for eco-nomic survival, cultic religion provided one way of preserving their integrity.

Other ways of maintaining their cultural values were available, and these proved more attractive than snake-handling to mountain people. The revival of interest in Appalachian music, whose antebellum origins have been discussed earlier, began about 1900 and merged into the handicraft revival of the 1920s.

Mountainous isolation had preserved traditional handicrafts, and when modern technology threatened to overwhelm them, Kentucky's Berea College fought to preserve traditional skills. In the late 1890s Berea featured courses in weaving taught by local craftsmen. Miss Frances L. Goodrich, a social worker with the Presbyterian Women's Board of Home Missions, came to the mountains just before the turn of the century and began to market quilts, coverlets, and homespun in the East.

This limited revival of weaving broadened during the next four decades. Two publication events marked the revival, and both owed their origins to the Russell Sage Foundation. Created in 1907 as part of the progressive impulse to improve living conditions in America, the foundation sponsored research and publications into a broad range of regional life. The first book was Cecil Sharp's *English Folk-Songs from the Southern Appalachians,* which appeared in 1917 under the imprint of the Oxford University Press. The second was Allen H. Eaton's *Handicrafts of the Southern Highlands* published by the Sage Foundation in 1937. Both men were introduced to the rich cultural legacy of Appalachia by Olive Dame Campbell, whose husband John had established and directed the Southern Highlands Division of the Sage Foundation for the eleven years that it operated as a distinct unit.

In 1923 Mrs. Campbell proposed the creation of a handicraft guild patterned on the ones she discovered in Finland during an extended study that she made of the folk revival in Denmark. She met Eaton in 1926 and invited him to address the annual Conference of Southern Mountain Workers. As a result of their mutual interest, they created the Southern Highland Handicraft Guild in December 1929.

The craft revival operated at three levels. First, it provided a critical source of revenue. By 1935 the handicraft revival had reached such proportions that Bertha M. Nienburg of the Women's Bureau of the Department of Labor published a bulletin on the subject. Based on research done in the summer of 1934 in mountain portions of Alabama, Georgia, Tennessee, Kentucky, Virginia, North Carolina, and West Virginia, the article identified one hundred five centers regularly employing craftsmen. Of the 15,000 estimated handicraft workers, 10,500 had actually earned money from their crafts during 1933. Some ninety-five percent of the workers who marketed their products through the centers were women, most of them working in their homes. These handicrafts sold for two-and-a-half million dollars in 1933, of which the craftsfolk received $520,000. Few of them earned the minimum wage for Southern factory workers ($12 per week or $600 for a fifty-week year). Both commercial and philanthropic outlets agreed that ten to twelve cents per hour was ample pay for craftswomen, whereas a rate of twenty to twenty-five cents was standard for men. Every one of the 563 handicraft workers interviewed for the survey stated that he or she worked to earn money as a chief or supplemental source of family income. The Bureau of Labor recommended that the newly organized Tennessee Valley Authority establish handicraft cooperatives to market the products at a rate more beneficial to the craftsmen and as a major alternative source of rural income.

Although this was the major short-range benefit of the revival, there were two more subtle results. People who had been led to believe that they were provincial, devoid of aesthetic sense, even barbaric, took pride in the fact that the products of their skilled hands were treasured by an increasingly standardized world. Whatever else could be said derogatory of hillbillies, no one could complain that "they take no pride in the things they make."

Third, America discovered Appalachia through mountain music. For millions of Americans who were too busy struggling through the depression to take much interest in quilts, it was the soulful sound of mountain music that left an Appalachian imprint. The sounds of twanging banjo or dulcimer had long echoed among the hills, but not until the twentieth century had serious researchers taken note. The dulcimer contained both melody and drone strings, which produced music suggestive of the haunting drone quality of the Scottish bagpipe, a sound which may have been its ancient inspiration. The traditional banjo featured a head of skin (cat, possum, raccoon, sheep, snake) and two or four strings; the most important innovation in the instrument was the appearance of a fifth or thumb string. Mountain pickers developed a unique, individualistic style utilizing the fifth string. Styles of playing, such as "frailing," were highly complex and learned exclusively from another player. Most of the musicians played by ear and minimized formal musical knowledge. Asked if they could read music, the standard reply was, "not enough to hurt my playing any." The banjos, songs, and styles changed little in the twentieth century, and five-string banjo music notation is nearly nonexistent. Like other parts of mountain culture, it was transmitted orally.

The lyric became an important way of communicating, and five-string banjo music oftentimes accompanied a message against the convict-lease system, tenant farming, or coal operators. Folklorist Archie Green has performed a notable service by connecting Appalachian musical score to protest lyric.

Before Green brought an academic perspective to the study of folk music, Alvin Pleasant Carter of Scott County, Virginia, spent the years between the world wars recording and popularizing tunes. One of Carter's songs, recorded in 1938, was entitled "Coal Miner's Blues":

> Some blues are just blues, mine are the miner's blues.
> Some blues are just blues, mine are the miner's blues.
> My troubles are coming by three and by twos.
>
> Blues and more blues, it's that coal black blues.
> Blues and more blues, it's that coal black blues.
> Got coal in my hair, got coal in my shoes.
>
> These blues are so blue, they are the coal black blues.
> These blues are so blue, they are the coal black blues.
> For my place will cave in, and my life I will lose.
>
> You say they are blues, these old miner's blues.
> You say they are blues, these old miner's blues.
> Now I must have sharpened these picks that I use.

I'm out with these blues, dirty coal black blues.
I'm out with these blues, dirty coal black blues.
We'll lay off tomorrow with the coal miner's blues.[5]

Carter, together with wife Sara and sister-in-law Maybelle, employed banjo, autoharp, and guitar to spread his repertoire in the 1920s and 1930s. Their first recording session in 1927 began careers that carried them across the United States playing and singing gospel songs, secular ballads, stories of unrequited love, cowboy and outlaw songs. They played an important role as collectors and transmitters, and they contributed to the Bluegrass style of playing as well as to the style of commercial country-western singers such as Johnny Cash and Merle Travis.

The revival of handicrafts and music continued and expanded in the 1970s. Appalachian folklore survived in Northern cities, and new journals popularized it in the mountains. The appearance of *Foxfire* Magazine at Rabun Gap, Georgia, in 1968, *Appalachian Journal* at Boone, North Carolina, in 1972, and *Appalachian Heritage* at Pippa Passes, Kentucky, in 1973 were symbolic of a new awareness that had begun with the handicraft and cultural revivals of the 1920s and 1930s.

The cultural revival in Appalachia helped clarify the options facing Southern poor whites. Progress might mean jobs and a better way of life to some, but to others it meant the extinction of old ways that were revered and still meaningful. Progress might mean the eradication of poor white racism and fundamentalism, but it would also spell doom to magnificent handicrafts and bonds of spirit and neighborliness by which people lived creatively with one another. In short, progress was not all good, and America had to learn to respect those who found the good life in a different sort of wisdom. For too long well-meaning people assumed that the poor did not know what was best for them; they concluded this partly because the poor did not always choose as they did. The poor must be saved from excessive individualism, racial prejudice, otherworldly religion, and rural-mindedness. Then, when attempts at reform met no enthusiasm and even occasional suggestions that social workers take their programs and go to hell, secular missionaries were disillusioned. White Southerners must share in the decisions affecting their destiny instead of entrusting their fate to bureaucrats, academicians, businessmen, power companies, and unions.

Just as black and Chicano studies served the object of consciousness raising among ethnics, so the emergence of redneck and hillbilly pride served a different type of ethnicity. Young people in Appalachia began to rediscover their own past, which made them less interested in aping the mainstream. Poor whites insisted that they too had a story to tell, a contribution to make.

Loyal Jones, director of the Appalachian Center at Berea College, was asked "What would you like to see happen in our land and people?" He captured the essence of the spirit of Appalachia, when he replied that he wanted to see "our people become free again and with free choices," to have rewarding work to do, and an income for those who could not labor. Mountain people in the past had sought freedom in isolation, which only bound them to misery and poverty. Modern culture now threatened them as much as the bulldozer:

> God A'mighty, we are in bad shape! And the worst thing of all is the realization that the ideals we cherish are long gone, except in our hearts. There is no way to go back to the way things were, though it would be good to go back. I yearn to roam the high coves of the Unakas again looking for squirrel or grouse, far from the sound of motors, or fish the clear Hiwassee of my childhood. But for me the freedom to do that is gone, even if there were a spot in the Unakas free from motors, or a clear Hiwassee. For all of us it has to be something new and different, but perhaps it can be for the same ideals—freedom, solitude, tradition, and control over our lives, in a relative sense at least.[6]

CHAPTER SEVEN

"A TIME TO WEEP, A TIME TO LAUGH..."

"For the needy shall not always be forgotten, and the hope of the poor shall not perish for ever." The promise of the Ninth Psalm provided comfort to generations of poor whites who read it by candlelight in simple cabins. Perhaps their grinding poverty reminded more affluent Americans of a different scripture, "The poor you have with you always. . . ."

Unfortunately, many Americans interpreted the latter verse as commandment rather than observation. Convinced that poverty was the result of sloth, lack of will, biological inferiority, or some equally unalterable condition, they prided themselves on their superior character. With remarkable equanimity they did forget the poor.

For those Americans who have remembered and attempted to help, the poor who were racial minorities and had suffered from historic discrimination were more easily discernible. The plight of those who had been persecuted systematically, seemed more explicable; but how could one explain poverty among Anglo-American whites who had never suffered such deprivations? They were not the persecuted; in fact, they seemed a culpable part of the white majority that had wronged blacks and other minorities.

The identity problems of poor whites were rooted in their similarity to people of higher station. Because they looked the same as middle and upper classes, shared common names, music, accents, religion, political parties, and often ancestors, it was easy to conclude that their lives were similar too. Subtle differences, which caused them to vote for "demagogic" politicians or worship in different churches even if members of the same denomination, seemed trivial.

Historians and other observers of the South may be forgiven for misunderstanding them, for Southern poor whites had little class perception of themselves. During the sectional controversy over slavery, they accepted and violently defended a system that unquestionably worked against their own economic self-interest.

Although the term "poor white" adequately expressed their economic condition, it never did justice to their rich culture. Negative stereotypes came to abound, charging Southern poor whites with moral degradation, the absence of aesthetic sensibility, excessive violence, and emotionalism. Yet, they produced beautiful crafts, ingenious folk architecture, humorous lore, and religious values that met their basic needs and provided a sense of personal worth.

Following the Civil War, poor whites entered the economic mainstream, producing coal, cotton, and clothing among other commercially marketable products. Their status became both more formal and more dependent as they drifted from subsistence living as hunters, fishermen, herdsmen, and small farmers to mining, mill work, and tenant farming. Their dependence on and proximity to more affluent Southerners reminded them of their deprivation and made them increasingly conscious of their common plight. Their protest, largely latent in the antebellum South, became more vociferous and better organized. As Grangers, Greenback-Laborites, Knights of Labor, and Populists they vainly sought power through cooperation. So desperate did they become, that on a few occasions some put aside racial animosity and joined with blacks in an attempt to wrest political control from conservative Democrats.

Wartime prosperity accomplished what biracial politics failed to do; it brought a better life, if only for awhile. New industry and record cotton prices provided unprecedented opportunities to poor whites between 1914 and 1919. Coupled with moderate political reforms enacted during the first decade and a half of the century, the improving economy brought substantial improvements in living conditions.

But good times did not last long. During the 1920s agricultural surpluses depressed the price of farm products, and the textile industry faltered. By the end of the decade, more than half the South's farmers were landless tenants, and hundreds of thousands of other Southerners barely survived as miners and mill operatives. The general prosperity of the decade once again made their declining fortunes harder to see or comprehend, and their racism divided them from possible allies among blacks who were deserting the land for urban jobs. Although a rich culture sustained them aesthetically and spiritually, they remained economically deprived and politically powerless.

In the midst of the tragic depression of the 1930s, Americans finally discovered white poverty. The discovery occurred partly because the poor began to make too much commotion to remain undetected. They joined labor unions, the Southern Tenant Farmers Union, and in a few instances, the Communist party. Intellectuals in the 1930s seemed fascinated by poor Southern whites, sometimes denigrating them and at other times celebrating their heroic struggle for survival. During the New Deal countless programs were devised by federal officials and implemented by idealistic social workers. Many were helpful but America possessed neither the will nor the resources to end poverty. Most of the South's white poor did not find prosperity at the end of a federal rainbow, but once again few of them sought solace in radical politics. Their succor came from traditional sources: family, religion, ties to land and community.

The attention that they received during the 1930s proved as transitory as it did illusory. Returning prosperity in the 1940s lowered a pale of obscurity across Southern poverty as Americans busied themselves with cosmic urgencies such as winning the war and reconstructing war-ravaged lands. Poland and China both seemed more immediate and relevant than Harlan County, U. S. A. Economic recovery that speeded the reconstruction of Germany and Japan worked its magic in the former Confederacy as well, and many Americans assumed that poverty, especially among whites, was a condition of the past. Flush with prosperity, they ignored less fortunate citizens. Neither labor unions nor federal programs alleviated the chronic poverty that stretched from the Potomac mud flats to the arid Southwestern deserts.

The promise of Psalms finally seemed to be realized in the springtime of the New Frontier. Once again intellectuals played a role in the new stirring of interest by publicizing conditions in the South. Poor whites also participated in the resurrection of concern by migrating northward in such large and disruptive numbers that they transformed a regional problem into a national one. A number of New Frontier programs were enacted under President Lyndon Baines Johnson, who often boasted of his own roots in the poor white frontier of central Texas.

One of the most ambitious federal projects was an attempt to rejuvenate Appalachia, which was one of the nation's oldest frontiers. This mountainous subregion differed substantially from other areas of the South, but shared an historic legacy of deprivation. Like other Southerners, mountain people were stereotyped in ways which made genuine understanding difficult. As before in the 1930s, the promise of federal largess was greater than the reality. Progress was made, but the nation never made the commitment of will or resources necessary to loosen the poverty that for so long had bound the poor.

Alleviating poverty among the South's neglected whites will be no easy undertaking; the partial failure of New Deal, Fair Deal, and New Frontier programs, all well-intentioned, emphasized the magnitude of the task. No single strategy will surmount the obstacles that are rooted in history and inherent in the region. Southern poor whites will have to change many traditional attitudes, especially the false racial pride that has bound them to a political and economic system that is antithetical to their interests. They must put aside their individualism at least enough to organize at the community level; labor unions, political pressure groups, activist churches could make local government more responsive to their needs.

But they also need help, and not all assistance can be expected from the government. Federal aid carries too many unacceptable strings ever to be accepted with equanimity. Southern poor whites resent condescension, and their folk traditions retain too much meaning to be submerged in federal homogeneity and blandness. Government can help, but the Southern landscape is littered with the wreckage of ill-conceived government panaceas.

Private business can be of immense help. New patterns of economic development have dispersed industry into the countryside where the needs are greatest. The advantages of the "sun belt" are obvious and need not include exploitation of labor. Markets and populations are growing faster in the South than elsewhere, the rural labor force is large and eager to work. Its historic individualism promises a minimum of friction with management if it is treated decently. If business approaches this challenge with no more social conscience than it did in the last third of the nineteenth century, or as it has more recently in the coal mines of Appalachia and the textile belt of the southern Piedmont, it will only multiply the problems. But enlightened capitalism can be a major factor in alleviating Southern poverty.

Perhaps no solution can end white poverty in the South. American society invariably attaches conditions to its offers of assistance. Many poor whites consider these demands for cultural conformity, whether expressed in the priority of highways to open Appalachia to travel and commerce or its propensity to ridicule Pentecostal religion, too extravagant a price to pay for material prosperity. As paradoxical as it must seem to most Americans, poor white culture demonstrates a relatedness and sense of meaning that they may not choose to risk for the alleged advantages of affluence. The real challenge before the nation is to offer decent opportunities while preserving as much as possible of traditional folkways. Such a strategy is impossible unless the mainstream recognizes the value of poor white culture, unless it acknowledges that it has as much to learn as it does to teach.

Bibliography

Unfortunately the literary birth rate among Southern historians approaches the legendary fertility of poor whites, and most of this academic output relates in one way or another to the subject of this book. One wavers between the temptation to name every book written on the South and listing nothing but the best and most relevant material. I have compromised, but this bibliography is closer to the second approach than the first. Therefore, I acknowledge my gratitude to U. B. Phillips and many unlisted historians, sociologists, economists, and folklorists, apologize to outraged specialists who note the absence of their favorite "saint," and plead guilty to many sins of omission.

In keeping with the format of this series, I have eliminated notes except for lengthy direct quotations. To compensate, I have attempted to emphasize interpretive debates and evaluative judgments in the bibliographical essay. It is hoped that the text will provide more pleasant reading for the interested layman, whereas the bibliography may provide the specialist with specific guides to further reading regarding conclusions encountered in the text. Consistent with the desire to provide a bibliography that will guide the reader to important interpretive discussions, I have organized the bibliography according to chapters.

1. *The Invisible Poor: Toward A Definition of Southern Poor Whites*

The best of many antebellum traveler's accounts of the Southern class structure was written by historian Frederick Law Olmsted, *A Journey in the Seaboard Slave States* (New York: Dix and Edwards, 1856). Olmsted's simplistic notion of a dichotomized society of aristocratic planters and poor whites was substantially modified by Frank L. Owsley in the

1940s. Owsley's work focused on the predominance of the yeoman class and deemphasized the extent of poor white influence. For an early statement of Owsley's research, see "The Pattern of Migration and Settlement on the Southern Frontier," *The Journal of Southern History,* XI (May, 1945), 147–176. His classic work was an elaboration of this earlier research entitled *Plain Folk of the Old South* (Baton Rouge: Louisiana State University Press, 1949).

Criticism of Owsley centered on two aspects of his thesis: the extent of the yeomanry and the degree of economic mobility in the 1850s. Two studies of individual counties (Hancock County, Georgia, and Harrison County, Texas) disputed Owsley's conclusions on both points: James C. Bonner, "Profile of a Late Ante-Bellum Community," *American Historical Review,* XLIX (July, 1944), 663–680; and Randolph B. Campbell, "Planters and Plain Folk: Harrison County, Texas, as a Test Case, 1850–1860," *The Journal of Southern History,* XL (August, 1974), 369–398. Two articles dealt more directly with Owsley's methodology, refuting some of it and modifying other portions. Fabian Linden attacked Owsley for defining farmer in such a narrow way as to eliminate approximately one-quarter of the rural white population: "Economic Democracy in the Slave South: An Appraisal of Some Recent Views," *The Journal of Negro History,* XXXI (April, 1946), 140–189. Gavin Wright modified Owsley's analysis of the 1850s by noting that the economic status of both the richest planters and the poorest whites declined relative to yeomen and small planters. Thus, the decade tended to reduce the gap between large and small planters and yeomen while the lot of the poor became worse relative to both yeomen and aristocracy: " 'Economic Democracy' and the Concentration of Agricultural Wealth in the Cotton South, 1850–1860," *Agricultural History,* XLIV (January, 1970), 63–93.

Differing views of Southern society came from pioneer Southern sociologist Howard Odum, "The Glory That Was and the Southern Grandeur That Was Not," *The Saturday Review of Literature,* XXVI (January 23, 1943), 9–10, 35–36, and from economist Peter Passell, "The Impact of Cotton Land Distribution on the Antebellum Economy," *Journal of Economic History,* XXXI (December, 1971), 917–937. Odum emphasized the diversity within the "third level" of society made up of poor Southern whites, thus offering one of the earliest challenges to the poor white stereotype. Passell developd the concept that land-intensive agriculture by planters intent on maximizing profits left a trail of worn-out land, which was farmed by poor whites. Elizabeth Wisner's *Social Welfare in the South: From Colonial Times to World War I* (Baton Rouge: Louisiana State University Press, 1970) provides examples of antebellum relief.

Marxist historian Eugene D. Genovese accepted Linden's criticism of the Owsley thesis and elaborated on that criticism. He rejected the notion of a flourishing livestock industry among yeomen in *The Political Economy of Slavery* (New York: Vintage Books, 1967), pp. 107–118, and traced Southern culture to "its discrete class roots" in an essay entitled "Potter and Woodward on the South," which appeared in a longer work entitled *In Red and Black: Marxian Explorations in Southern and Afro-American History* (New York, Vintage Books, 1968), pp. 299–314. In his more recent *Roll, Jordan, Roll* (New York: Pantheon Books, 1974), Genovese elaborated the complexity of poor white-black relations, claiming that despite poor white racism, there also were instances of cooperation (see especially pp. 22–25).

Recent studies have challenged Genovese's conclusions in much the same way he questioned Owsley's. Carl Degler disputed Genovese's emphasis on planter coherence in his book *The Other South: Southern Dissenters in the Nineteenth Century* (New York: Harper and Row, 1974). A recent essay by Forrest McDonald and Grady McWhiney challenged Genovese by focusing attention on the huge herds of swine and the professional herdsmen who drove them. Although they appeared to be poor, they possessed considerable wealth in livestock, and were therefore substantially more prosperous than Genovese claimed: "The Ante-bellum Southern Herdsman: A Reinterpretation," *The Journal of Southern History*, XLI (May, 1975), 147–166.

For an excellent summary of Genovese's role in the debate over the antebellum Southern class structure, see Robert E. Shalhope, "Race, Class, Slavery and the Ante-bellum Southern Mind," *The Journal of Southern History*, XXXVII (November, 1971), 557–574.

Two additional works analyzed class divisions in very different ways. A highly controversial study by Robert Williams Fogel and Stanley L. Engerman used computer analysis to argue that as a whole white Southerners compared favorably with Northerners in the distribution of wealth: *Time on the Cross: The Economics of American Negro Slavery* (Boston: Little, Brown and Co., 1974). Hugh C. Bailey offered a valuable insight into the mind of the remarkable Hinton Helper. Born in poverty, Helper concluded that slavery had produced a caste system by which a favored few exploited the masses. Helper, though himself a racist, advocated the abolition of slavery: Hugh C. Bailey, *Hinton Rowan Helper: Abolitionist-Racist* (Tuscaloosa: University of Alabama Press, 1965).

One of the most useful studies of antebellum whites, though limited to four states, was authored by Rudolph M. Lapp: "The Ante Bellum Poor Whites of the South Atlantic States," Ph.D. dissertation in history, University of California at Berkeley, 1945. It was a major corrective to Owsley's study, estimating the number of poor whites to have been much higher. The reason poor whites seemed to have disappeared in the 1850s was explained partly by their migration to towns. Also, many female heads of families preferred not to be listed in the census as unemployed, and listed their occupation as "seamstress," a term which almost always was a census euphemism for "poor." Another dissertation that emphasized the role of technology in perpetuating poverty was economist Lee S. Balliet's "Anglo Poverty in the Rural South," Ph.D. dissertation in economics, University of Texas at Austin, 1974.

Sociologist Mildred Mell attributed the origins of poor white culture to the fact that, alone among whites, they stood outside the economic system until after the Civil War. Developing her theory first in her doctoral dissertation in 1938, "A Definitive Study of the Poor Whites of the South," University of North Carolina at Chapel Hill, she later popularized her ideas in a number of journal articles. Two excellent summaries of her thesis were: "Poor Whites of the South," *Social Forces,* XVII (December, 1938), 153–167; "The Southern Poor White: Myth, Symbol, and Reality of a Nation," *The Saturday Review of Literature,* XXVI (January 23, 1943), 13–15.

The stereotype of the Southern poor white has been the subject of several articles. Edgar T. Thompson incorporated many of the popular connotations of that phrase in his article, "Purpose and Tradition in Southern Rural Society: A Point of View for Research," *Social Forces,* XXV (March, 1947), 270–280. A much more useful article on the origin and function of the term "cracker" was written by Mozell C. Hill and Bevode C. McCall: " 'Cracker Culture': A Preliminary Definition," *Phylon,* XI (Third Quarter, 1950), 223–231.

Poor whites shared some attitudes with their more affluent neighbors. One example was their scorn for physical labor. The implications of this view are discussed in David Bertelson, *The Lazy South* (New York: Oxford University Press, 1967). Another example was the almost universal racist assumption of whites toward blacks. Useful surveys of racial thought, and the poor white role in it, are: W. J. Cash, *The Mind of the South* (New York: Alfred A. Knopf, 1941); W. P. Brown, "Role of the Poor Whites in Race Contacts of the South," *Social Forces,* XIX (December, 1940), 258–268; and James W. Vander Zanden, "The Ideology of White Supremacy," *Journal of the History of Ideas,* XX (June-September, 1959), 385–402.

On issues other than race, whites in the antebellum South frequently divided along class lines. For the steady expansion of democracy, especially in the new states of the Southwest, see: Fletcher M. Green, "Democracy in the Old South," *The Journal of Southern History,* XII (February, 1946), 3–23; and Clement Eaton, "Class Differences in the Old South," *The Virginia Quarterly Review,* XXXIII (Summer, 1957), 357–370. For more specific examples of class appeal by demagogues to poor whites, see: Paul H. Buck, "The Poor Whites of the Ante-Bellum South," *The American Historical Review,* XXXI (October, 1925), 41–54; Edwin A. Miles, "Franklin E. Plummer: Piney Woods Spokesman of the Jackson Era," *Journal of Mississippi History,* XIV (January, 1952), 1–34; and Reinhard H. Luthin, "Some Demagogues in American History," *The American Historical Review,* LVII (October, 1951), 22–46.

The extent of class division in one state was the topic of Roger W. Shugg's book, *Origins of Class Struggle in Louisiana: A Social History of White Farmers and Laborers During Slavery and After, 1840–1875* (Baton Rouge: Louisiana State University Press, 1939). Some victories resulting from poor white political activity came in the creation of public welfare and education programs: Charles Sydnor, *The Development of Southern Sectionalism, 1819–1848* (Baton Rouge: Louisiana State University Press, 1948), especially pp. 60–63; and Maybelle Coleman, "Poverty and Poor Relief in the Plantation Society of South Carolina: A Study in the Sociology of a Social Problem," Ph.D. dissertation in sociology, Duke University, 1943. Leah Atkins dealt with a more significant aspect of lower-class influence on politics, the Southern campaign for free land: Leah Rawls Atkins, "Southern Congressmen and the Homestead Bill," Ph.D. dissertation in history, Auburn University, 1974. Also useful was Atkins' essay, "Williamson R. W. Cobb and the Graduation Act of 1854," *The Alabama Review,* XXVIII (January, 1975), 16–31. Historian John Hope Franklin questioned the extent of lower-class reform, noting that the South ended the antebellum period largely without public welfare programs: "Public Welfare in the South During the Reconstruction Era, 1865–1880," *The Social Science Review,* XLIV (December, 1970), 379–392.

2. *Dogtrots and Jack Tales:*
Toward a Definition of Poor White Culture

Studies of antebellum folk culture are less numerous than the historical literature devoted to politics and economics, but the available material is provocative and important. William R. Ferris, Jr., authored some excellent exploratory essays in Southern folk architecture: "American Folklore" and "Don't Throw it Away," *Yale Alumni Magazine,* XXXVI and XXXVII (May, 1973, and March, 1974), 10–17 and 20–22; "Mississippi Folk

Architecture: A Sampling," *Mid-South Folklore*, I (Winter, 1973), 71–84; "The Shotgun, the Dogtrot, and the Row House," *Southern Voices*, I (May/June, 1974), 28–32.

A more familiar aspect of folk culture concerned humorists of the Old Southwest whose work both recorded and described poor white culture. Ardrey Shields McIlwaine's 1937 dissertation in English at the University of Chicago, "The Southern Poor-White: A Literary History," was published in altered form under the title *The Southern Poor-White: From Lubberland to Tobacco Road* (Norman: University of Oklahoma Press, 1939). The best of the antebellum humorists preserved many of the tall tales, exaggerations, and hero stories of poor whites. I relied on Augustus Baldwin Longstreet's *Georgia Scenes* (New York: Harper and Brothers, 1840), especially his essay entitled "The Fight," pp. 53–64; David Crockett, *The Life of David Crockett* (New York: A. L. Burt, 1903), especially his famous "bear hunt" chapters, pp. 122–150; and Johnson J. Hooper, *Simon Suggs' Adventures* (Americus, Georgia: Americus Book Co., 1928). Two folklorists probed these themes as they applied to poor whites and concluded that the humorists captured universal themes which had long circulated orally among common folk: James T. Pearce, "Folk Tales of the Southern Poor-Whites, 1820–1860," *Journal of American Folklore*, 63 (October-December, 1950), 398–412; James H. Penrod, "Folk Motifs in Old Southwestern Humor," *Southern Folklore Quarterly*, XIX (June, 1955), 117–124. Both articles were provocative, although Pearce strays a bit far in his conclusion that the repetition of tales "show that the poor white was an intellectually listless person" (p. 398). Avery Craven traced the humorous character traits of poor whites to the frontier quality of Southern life: Avery Craven, "The 'Turner Theories' and the South," *The Journal of Southern History*, V (August, 1939), 291–314.

There is a rich literature on Southern folk music thanks largely to the remarkable George Pullen Jackson. Boston-born, Jackson lived in Birmingham, Alabama, before taking a Ph.D. in Germany and returning to become head of the German department at Vanderbilt University in Nashville, Tennessee. He made his major contribution not in his own academic area but in the rich fasola music tradition of the rural southern Highlands. For an excellent introduction, see Jackson's "Some Factors in the Diffusion of American Religious Folksongs," *Journal of American Folklore*, LXV (October-December, 1952), 365–369; *The Story of the Sacred Harp, 1844–1944* (Nashville: Vanderbilt University Press, 1944); and *White Spirituals of the Southern Uplands: The Story of the Fasola Folk, Their Songs, Singings, and "Buckwheat Notes"* (Chapel Hill: University of North Carolina Press, 1933). The secular ballad tradition in the southern Appalachians was explained best by Evelyn Kendrick Wells, *The Ballad Tree: A Study of British and American Ballads, their Folklore, Verse, and Music* (New York: Ronald Press Co., 1950), especially the chapters concerning Francis James Child and Cecil Sharp. The seminal work on this topic is Cecil Sharp, *English Folk Songs from The Southern Appalachians,* Vols. I and II (London: Oxford University Press, 1952, originally published in 1917). Loman D. Cansler wrote an excellent essay on the significance of ballads in understanding folk culture entitled "What Folksongs Reveal About Our Cultural Heritage," *Southern Folklore Quarterly,* XX (June, 1956), 126–129.

The fasola tradition of music played an important role in antebellum revivalistic religion. Dickson D. Bruce, Jr., has produced an analysis of shaped-note lyrics in his *And They All Sang Hallelujah: Plain-Folk Camp-Meeting Religion, 1800–1845* (Knoxville: University of Tennessee Press, 1974). Unfortunately, Bruce was confused by Frank L. Owsley's definition of Plain Folk and tried, unsuccessfully, to exclude poor whites from his designation. Numerous scholars, however, emphasized the class appeal of the religious themes that Bruce described, noting, for instance, that the antimissionary movement and especially Primitive Baptists appealed mainly to poor whites. For examples, see the works of Mozell C. Hill, Bevode C. McCall, and Rudolph M. Lapp, referred to earlier. By far the most useful analysis of this subject was an essay by Bertram Wyatt-Brown entitled "The Antimission Movement in the Jacksonian South: A Study in Regional Folk Culture," *The Journal of Southern History,* XXXVI (November, 1970), 501–529. Also helpful was Richard A. Humphrey's essay entitled "Development of Religion in Southern Appalachia: The Personal Quality," *Appalachian Journal,* 1 (Spring, 1974), 244–254. John B. Boles traced the Southern evangelical mind back to the great religious revivals of the early nineteenth century in his study, *The Great Revival, 1787–1805: The Origins of the Southern Evangelical Mind* (Lexington: University of Kentucky Press, 1972). Barton W. Stone's *The Biography of Eld. Barton Warren Stone, Written By Himself: With Additions and Reflections by John Rogers* (New York: Arno Press, 1972) was a reprint of Stone's account of Cane Ridge and a significant insight into the doctrinal basis of the Great Revival. David Edwin Harrell, Jr., emphasized the lower-class antebellum orientation of the Disciples of Christ in his *Quest for a Christian America* (Saint Louis, Missouri: Bethany Press, 1966).

David M. Potter's *The South and the Sectional Conflict* (Baton Rouge: Louisiana State University Press, 1968) was a stimulating interpretive reference for this entire essay. Potter's thesis in his chapter entitled "The Enigma of the South" was that Southern folk culture had a relatedness and purposefulness that caused it to endure even in the face of mass industrial culture.

3. "Lint Heads" and "Diggers": The Forgotten People of the New South, 1865–1920

Many monographs treated the subject of Reconstruction, but one of the most useful descriptions of the destitution of poor whites was an older work by Walter L. Fleming, *The Sequel of Appomattox* (New Haven: Yale University Press, 1926), pp. 12–16. A Northern view that embodied a "poor white trash" stereotype was written by Freedmen's Bureau official John William De Forest. An excellent summary is found in James Davidson, "The Post-Bellum Poor-White As Seen by J. W. De Forest," *Southern Folklore Quarterly*, XXIV (June, 1960), 101–108. A recent study of Reconstruction that mentioned the class origins of white terrorism in Florida was Jerrell H. Shofner's *Nor Is It Over Yet: Florida in the Era of Reconstruction, 1863–1877* (Gainesville: The University Presses of Florida, 1974), especially pp. 228–231.

The South had a primitive system of public welfare services before 1865, which the Reconstruction regimes expanded rapidly. The most useful studies examined for this topic were: John Hope Franklin, "Public Welfare in the South During the Reconstruction Era, 1865–80," *The Social Service Review*, XLIV (December, 1970), 379–392; and the works of Maybelle Coleman and Mildred Mell, cited earlier.

Many excellent works treated the problems of the South's tenant farmers. For discussions of the origins of the tenant system, I relied on: Thomas D. Clark, "Southern Common Folk After The Civil War," *The South Atlantic Quarterly*, XLIV (April, 1945), 130–145; and Wilson Gee, "The Distinctiveness of Southern Culture," *The South Atlantic Quarterly*, XXXVIII (April, 1939), 119–129. A useful perspective on the evolution of tenancy was provided by geographer Merle Prunty, Jr., "The Renaissance of the Southern Plantation," *The Geographical Review*, XLV (October, 1955), 459–491. Agricultural historian Stephen J. DeCanio contends that the least productive farmer in the South was the white noncotton farmer who tilled the worst Southern soil: *Agriculture in the Postbellum South: The Economics of Production and Supply* (Cambridge: Massachusetts Institute of Technology Press, 1974). Although some blacks were more productive than white tenants, they were treated worse by white landowners: Roger Ranson and Richard Sutch, "Debt Peonage in the Cotton South after the Civil War," *Journal of Economic History*, XXXII (September, 1972), 641–669.

There are several excellent discussions of poor white health: Daphne A. Roe, *A Plague of Corn: The Social History of Pellagra* (Ithaca: Cornell University Press, 1973); Elizabeth W. Etheridge, *The Butterfly Caste: A Social History of Pellagra in the South* (Westport: Greenwood Publishing Corporation, 1972). The most intriguing thesis, however, was found in an article on clay-eating: Robert W. Twyman, "The Clay Eater: A New Look at an Old Southern Enigma," *The Journal of Southern History,* XXXVII (August, 1971), 439–448.

The life and culture of poor whites was a mixture of tragedy and hope. They developed institutions, crafts, and arts, which have attracted much recent attention. Among the most useful scholarly studies were Calvin Claudel, "The Folktales of Louisiana and Their Background," *Southern Folklore Quarterly,* XIX (September, 1955), 164–170; Vallie T. White, "Some Folktales from North Louisiana," *Southern Folklore Quarterly,* XX (September, 1956), 164–177; and Ray B. Browne, *Popular Beliefs and Practices from Alabama* (Berkeley: University of California Press, 1958).

Monographic literature about Southern industrial laborers has grown steadily in the past two decades making it difficult to understand the general neglect of this subject by textbooks and general histories of the South. The addition of white immigrants to the South's industrial classes is discussed in a number of articles: Rowland T. Berthoff, "Southern Attitudes Toward Immigration, 1865–1914," *The Journal of Southern History,* XVII (February, 1951), 328–360; Richard J. Hopkins, "Occupational and Geographical Mobility in Atlanta, 1870–1896," *The Journal of Southern History,* XXXIV (May, 1968), 200–213; two articles by Durward Long treated immigrants and labor problems in the city of Tampa: "An Immigrant Co-operative Medicine Program in the South, 1887–1963," *The Journal of Southern History,* XXXI (November, 1965), 417–434; and "Labor Relations in the Tampa Cigar Industry, 1885–1911," *Labor History,* XII (Fall, 1971), 551–559.

The best-known survey of organized labor in the South was F. Ray Marshall's *Labor in the South* (Cambridge: Harvard University Press, 1967). A brief survey entitled "Development of Trade-Unionism in the South," authored by H. M. Douty, can be found in *Monthly Labor Review,* LXIII (October, 1946), 555–582. For the textile industry, the most useful work is a revisionist study of the Knights of Labor in the South by Melton A. McLaurin, *Paternalism and Protest: Southern Cotton Mill Workers and Organized Labor, 1875–1905* (Westport, Connecticut: Greenwood Publishing Corporation, 1971). By pushing the date of active unionism back into the 1870s, McLaurin has documented the early rise of class consciousness among the poor whites. Katherine A. Harvey, "The Knights of Labor in the Maryland Coal Fields, 1878–1882," *Labor History,* X (Fall, 1969), 555–583, complemented the McLaurin study. For the political involvement of the Knights of Labor in Jacksonville, Florida, see: J. Wayne Flynt, *Duncan Upshaw Fletcher: Dixie's Reluctant Progressive* (Tallahassee: Florida State University Press, 1971), pp. 10–20; and Edward N. Akin, "When A Minority Becomes the Majority: Blacks in Jacksonville Politics, 1887–1907," *The Florida Historical Quarterly,* LIII (October, 1974), 123–145. Kate Born discussed the growth of labor influence in Memphis in an article entitled "Organized Labor in Memphis, Tennessee, 1826–1901," *The West Tennessee Historical Society Papers,* XXI (1967), 60–79. Child labor, one of the most tragic problems introduced by industrialism, was the focus of William I. Trattner's volume, *Crusade for the Children: A History of the National Child Labor Committee and Child Labor Reform in America* (Chicago: Quadrangle Books, 1970). A splendid study of many aspects of Southern labor is entitled *Essays in Southern Labor History: Selected Papers, Southern Labor History Conference, 1976,* edited by Gary M. Fink and Merl E. Reed (Westport, Connecticut: Greenwood Press, 1977). This volume contains essays on the Knights of Labor in the South, the textile organizing effort, the coal strikes in West Virginia, and labor conflict in the oil fields and among urban transportation workers.

It has been argued repeatedly that poor white racism precluded the development of class consciousness. Poverty-stricken whites would not cooperate with blacks even in their mutual self-interest. While there is some truth to the charge, there is much evidence of interracial cooperation along class lines among Southern workers. A sample follows that heavily influenced the interpretations of class consciousness found in this chapter: Herbert G. Gutman, "Black Coal Miners and the Greenback-Labor Party in Redeemer Alabama: 1878–1879," *Labor History,* X (Summer, 1969), 506–535; Paul Worthman, "Black Workers and Labor Unions in Birmingham, Alabama, 1879–1904," *Labor History,* X (Summer, 1969), 375–407; George T. Morgan, Jr., "No Compromise—No Recognition: John Henry Kirby, the Southern Lumber Operators' Association, and Unionism in the Piney Woods," *Labor History,* X (Spring, 1969), 193–204. Two excellent articles by Merl E. Reed examined this theme among Texas and Louisiana poor whites and blacks: "Lumberjacks and Longshoremen: The I. W. W. in Louisiana," *Labor History,* XIII (Winter, 1972), 41–59; and "The I.W.W. and Individual Freedom in Western Louisiana, 1913," *Louisiana History,* X (Winter, 1969), 61–69. Another study of biracial cooperation among radical Texas and Louisiana timber workers was James R. Green, "The Brotherhood of Timber Workers, 1910–1913: A Radical Response to Industrial Capitalism in the Southern U.S.A.," *Past and Present,* Number 60 (August, 1973), 161–200. An extremely useful monograph on biracial cooperation among Alabama coal miners was Robert David Ward and William W. Rogers: *Labor Revolt in Alabama: The Great Strike of 1894* (Tuscaloosa: University of Alabama Press, 1965).

The historiography of the Populist movement is rich, having attracted the attention of some of the nation's finest historians. The interpretive perspective, which I have adopted, was summarized best by Norman Pollack, *The Populist Response to Industrial America* (Cambridge: Harvard University Press, 1962). The best study of the Farmers' Alliance, which preceded the Populist party, is Robert C. McMath, Jr., *Populist Vanguard: A History of the Southern Farmers' Alliance* (Chapel Hill: University of North Carolina Press, 1975). Michael Schwartz in *Radical Protest and Social Structure: The Southern Farmers' Alliance and Cotton Tenancy, 1880–1890* (New York: Academic Press, 1976) stresses class conflict within the leadership of the Alliance. Tracing the origin of the Alliance to the exploitation of tenants and other economic factors, his class conflict hypothesis is a corrective for historians who seem to be incapable of separating the conservative and liberal wings of the farmers' movement. Of the many studies on the state level, the most useful were: W. I. Hair, *Bourbonism and Agrarian Protest: Louisiana Politics,* 1877–1900 (Baton Rouge: Louisiana State University Press, 1969); Roger W. Shugg, *Origins of Class Struggle in Louisiana: A Social History of White Farmers and Laborers during Slavery and After, 1840–1875* (Baton Rouge: Louisiana State University Press, 1939); and William W. Rogers, *The One-Gallused Rebellion: Agrarianism in Alabama, 1865–1896* (Baton Rouge: Louisiana State University Press, 1970). For a sample of a view of the Populists that deemphasized class notions, see Sheldon Hackney, *Populism to Progressivism in Alabama* (Princeton: Princeton University Press, 1969).

Many other works give insight into the growth of class conflict among Southern farmers. The most useful for this study were: Theodore Saloutos, *Farmer Movements in the South, 1865–1933* (Lincoln: University of Nebraska Press, 1960); two works by C. Vann Woodward, *Origins of the New South, 1877–1913* (Baton Rouge: Louisiana State University Press, 1951), and *Tom Watson: Agrarian Rebel* (New York: MacMillan Co., 1938); Paul J. Vanderwood, *Night Riders of Reelfoot Lake* (Memphis: Memphis State University Press, 1969); John G. Miller, *The Black Patch War* (Chapel Hill: The University of North Carolina Press, 1936); James O. Nall, *The Tobacco Night Riders of Kentucky and Tennessee, 1905–1909* (Louisville, Kentucky: The Standard Press, 1939).

Another point of controversy has been the interaction of evangelical religion and white reform movements. The traditional view maintained that evangelicals held themselves out of the Populist movement: Rufus Spain, *At Ease in Zion: A Social History of Southern Baptists, 1865–1900* (Nashville: Vanderbilt University Press, 1967); John Lee Eighmy, *Churches in Cultural Captivity: A History of the Social Attitudes of Southern Baptists* (Knoxville: University of Tennessee Press, 1972); Frederick A. Bode, "Religion and Class Hegemony: A Populist Critique in North Carolina," *The Journal of Southern History,* XXXVII (August, 1971), 417–438; John Hope Franklin, "The Great Confrontation: The South and the Problem of Change," *The Journal of Southern History,* XXXVIII (February, 1972), 3–20. The problem with these evaluations was their elitist orientation. They based their judgments on convention-wide leadership, pastors of large churches, and denominational newspapers. They ignored sectarianism and the smaller churches in rural areas. A suggestion of the cleavage can be seen in the religious folklore recorded by Vance Rudolph, "Tales From Arkansas," *Southern Folklore Quarterly,* XIX (June, 1955), 125–136. In their studies of Populism, both W. I. Hair and W. W. Rogers noted the impact of evangelical religion on the Populist movements in Alabama and Louisiana. Most importantly, however, my own reading in the primary sources of Baptist history revealed substantial division within that denomination on the issues raised by Populists. Robert C. McMath, Jr., defined the evangelical ambivalence toward agrarian protest (see chapter XI, "The Alliance and Southern Protestantism," in "The Farmers' Alliance in the South: The Career of an Agrarian Institution," Ph.D. dissertation in history, University of North Carolina at Chapel Hill, 1972). Garin Burbank's study of Oklahoma Socialism, *When Farmers Voted Red: The Gospel of Socialism in the Oklahoma Countryside, 1910–1924* (Westport, Conn.: Greenwood Press, 1976) maintains that rural Protestantism was transformed into a millennarian and transcendent faith in the possibility of universal economic cooperation. This transformation was brought about by Socialist-minded ministers utilizing the techniques and idiom of rural Christianity. Most of the Socialist vote came from rural areas with high rates of farm tenancy.

Even the evangelical elite took more interest in poor whites and their problems than most historians have given them credit. This limited concern has been a particular interest of mine in several articles that modify the traditional otherworldly view of Southern evangelicals: J. Wayne Flynt, "Organized Labor, Reform, and Alabama Politics, 1920," *The Alabama Review,* XXIII (July, 1970), 163–180; "Alabama White Protestantism and Labor, 1900–1914," *The Alabama Review,* XXV (July, 1972), 192–217; "Baptists and Reform," *Baptist History and Heritage,* VII (October, 1972),

211–222; "Dissent in Zion: Alabama Baptists and Social Issues, 1900–1914," *The Journal of Southern History*, XXXV (November, 1969), 523–542. William W. Rogers and I also noted the significance of religious backgrounds of prominent Alabama Populist orators: "Reform Oratory in Alabama, 1890–1896," *The Southern Speech Journal*, XXIX (Winter, 1963), 94–106.

Several of my students and former students have broadened this topic with helpful studies: Martha L. Lanier, "Alabama Methodists and Social Issues, 1900–1914," M.A. thesis in history, Samford University, 1969; Billy Frank Sumners, "The Social Attitudes of Southern Baptists Toward Certain Issues, 1910–1920," M.A. thesis in history, University of Texas at Arlington, 1975.

Archie Green has performed a great service by calling attention to an important new source of primary information on poor white culture. For a good sample of Green's work, see *Only A Miner: Studies in Recorded Coal-Mining Songs* (Urbana: University of Illinois Press, 1972). Even more useful for its musical recordings taken from the Library of Congress is a tape of an interview with Green: "Folklore of the American Labor Movement," Pacific Tape Library, 5316 Venice Boulevard, Los Angeles, California, 90019.

The demagogues spawned by the Populist awakening championed poor white economic interests, but they also unleashed a torrent of racism and violence. The class implications of their rise to power are discussed in Dewey Grantham's *The Democratic South* (Athens: University of Georgia Press, 1963); A. D. Kirwan's *Revolt of the Rednecks: Mississippi Politics, 1876–1925* (Lexington: University of Kentucky Press, 1951); Charles S. Sydnor, "Democrats, Demagogues, and Negroes," *The South Atlantic Quarterly*, XLIX (October, 1950), 507–513; and Lewis P. Jones, "Word War Between Cole Blease and the Gonzales," *South Carolina History Illustrated*, I (May, 1970), 4–12. Studies that dealt with poor white violence and racism include: Lawrence J. Friedman, *The White Savage: Racial Fantasies in the Postbellum South* (Englewood Cliffs: Prentice-Hall, 1970); William F. Holmes, "Whitecapping: Agrarian Violence in Mississippi, 1902–1906," *The Journal of Southern History*, XXXV (May, 1969), 165–185; Jack Temple Kirby, *Darkness at the Dawning: Race and Reform in the Progressive South* (New York: J. B. Lippincott Company, 1972); Arthur F. Raper, *The Tragedy of Lynching* (Chapel Hill: The University of North Carolina Press, 1933); William R. Ferris, Jr., "Racial Stereotypes In White Folklore," *Keystone Folklore Quarterly*, (Winter Issue, 1970), 188–198; and the Southern Commission on the Study of Lynching, *Lynchings and What They Mean* (Atlanta: The Commission, 1931).

Of the many tapes in the Samford University Oral History Collection that recorded the experiences of poor whites, three were most important for this chapter: folk medicine practitioner "Aunt" Jessie Thrasher, interviewed at McCalla, Alabama, on November 12, 1974; coal miner Elmer Burton, interviewed in Walker County, Alabama, on December 3, 1974; and textile worker Mrs. L. A. House, interviewed in Sylacauga, Alabama, on July 10, 1974.

4. *Progress and Poverty, Southern Style: The 1920s and 1930s*

The starting place for anyone interested in the South since 1920 is George B. Tindall's masterful *The Emergence of the New South, 1913–1945* (Baton Rouge: Louisiana State University Press, 1967). Professor Tindall's own roots in the textile town of Greenville, South Carolina, made him unusually sensitive to poor whites and the economic struggles of the 1920s and 1930s. His perception of the role of religion in poor white culture is more useful than Woodward's analysis for the pre–1920s period that appeared in *Origins of the New South, 1877–1913*. Although Tindall summarized the argument of the "benighted South" in his book, more detailed treatments are found in Tindall's "The Benighted South: Origins of a Modern Image," *The Virginia Quarterly Review*, XL (1964), 281–294; and "The 'Colonial Economy' and the Growth Psychology: The South in the 1930's," *The South Atlantic Quarterly*, LXIV (Autumn, 1965), 464–477. Cash's *The Mind of the South* is seminal, and several essay length reviews are helpful: Louis D. Rubin, Jr., "The Mind of the South," *The Sewanee Review,* LXII (October-December, 1954), C. Vann Woodward, "W. J. Cash Reconsidered," *New York Times Review of Books,* December 4, 1969.

Since this chapter arbitrarily omits Appalachia, which will be discussed separately, poor whites during this period can be grouped into two basic occupational categories: textile workers and tenant farmers. The plight of tenant farmers attracted the most attention from journalists, academicians, and novelists. General information on health, diet, land conditions, and fertility rates casts the economic crisis in a much wider context: Bernice Milburn Moore, "Present Status and Future Trends in the Southern White Family," *Social Forces,* XVI (March, 1938), 406–410; Arthur Raper, "Gullies and What They Mean," *Social Forces,* XXIII (May, 1945), 451–459. Economic conditions among Southern tenant farmers were well documented in many polemical works produced in the 1930s as well as by more recent and dispassionate scholarship: Will Alexander, Charles S. Johnson, and Edwin D. Embree, *The Collapse of Cotton Tenancy: A Sum-*

mary of Field Studies and Statistical Surveys, 1933–35 (Chapel Hill: University of North Carolina Press, 1935); David Eugene Conrad, *The Forgotten Farmers: The Story of Sharecroppers in the New Deal* (Urbana: University of Illinois Press, 1965); two works by William H. Nicholls, "The South as a Developing Area," *The Journal of Politics,* XXVI (February, 1964), 22–40, and *Southern Tradition and Regional Progress* (Chapel Hill: University of North Carolina Press, 1960); J. Allen Tower, "Cotton Change in Alabama, 1879–1946," *Economic Geography,* XXVI (January, 1950), 6–28; Rupert B. Vance and Nadia Danilevsky, "Population and the Pattern of Unemployment in the Southeast, 1930–1937," *Southern Economic Journal,* VII (July, 1940), 187–203; Franklin C. Erickson, "The Broken Cotton Belt," *Economic Geography,* XXIV (October, 1948), 263–268. The most important event in popularizing the extent of the agrarian tragedy came in 1937 with the publication of the presidential committee report: *Farm Tenancy: Message From the President of the United States Transmitting the Report of the Special Committee on Farm Tenancy,* House Document No. 149, 75th Congress, 1937. A moving portrait of tenant women is found in Margaret Jarman Hagood, *Mothers of the South: Portraiture of the White Tenant Farm Women* (Chapel Hill: University of North Carolina Press, 1939). An equally evocative work produced by the Federal Writers' Project under the editorial direction of W. T. Couch was entitled *These Are Our Lives* (Chapel Hill: University of North Carolina Press, 1939), and allowed the poor to tell their own stories.

During recent years increasing criticism has been directed toward the New Deal for ignoring the problems of the poorest Americans, an argument raised as early as the 1930s by the Southern Tenant Farmers' Union. A 1942 University of North Carolina dissertation in sociology by Selz Cabot Mayo, "Rural Poverty and Relief in the Southeast, 1933–1935," concentrated on the temporary relief aspects of the early New Deal as well as long range implications of rehabilitation policy. An impressive array of statistical charts documented the vast amount of relief, although it obviously was a stopgap program not designed to cure basic ills. An excellent dissertation in 1972 by historian Paul Eric Mertz at the University of Oklahoma, " 'Economic Problem No. 1,' The New Deal and Southern Poverty," provided a legislative history of New Deal measures designed to help the poverty South, but concluded that the New Deal left the task of eliminating poverty undone. James G. Maddox traced the development of the major New Deal agency to attempt the task of eradicating tenancy in a 1950 Harvard University dissertation, "The Farm Security Administration." Agricultural historian Theodore Saloutos defended the New Deal and emphasized its concern for the rural poor in an important essay rebutting revisionist arguments: "New Deal Agricultural Policy: An Evaluation," *The Journal of American History*, LXI (September, 1974), 394–416.

The Southern Tenant Farmers' Union has attracted major attention because of its left-of-center criticism of the Department of Agriculture and New Deal agricultural policies. For a survey of the S.T.F.U., see Donald H. Grubbs, *Cry From the Cotton: The Southern Tenant Farmers' Union and the New Deal* (Chapel Hill: University of North Carolina Press, 1971). To gain perspective on S.T.F.U. leader H. L. Mitchell, I relied heavily on "The Reminiscences of H. L. Mitchell," Oral History Research Office, Columbia University, 1957; H. L. Mitchell and J. R. Butler, "The Cropper Learns His Fate," *The Nation*, CXLI (September 18, 1935), 328–329; and several personal interviews with "Mitch," especially a lengthy discussion of rural religion among S.T.F.U. members and organizers on April 21, 1972, in Birmingham, Alabama. Other useful essays on Southern tenant farmers include: M. S. Venkataramani, "Norman Thomas, Arkansas Sharecroppers, and the Roosevelt Agricultural Policies, 1933–1937," *The Mississippi Valley Historical Review*, XLVII (September, 1960), 224–246; Jerold S. Auerbach, "Southern Tenant Farmers: Socialist Critics of the New Deal," *Labor History*, VII (Winter, 1966), 3–18. Auerbach denied that the S.T.F.U. was as genuinely interracial as Grubbs believed and further contended that it was resisted no more violently than most other unions in the South. In fact, he interpreted the union more as a broad protest movement closely linked to the Socialist party than as a labor organization.

Other New Deal measures affected the South, though none so broadly as agricultural policy. Conditions in the textile mills are summarized by Tindall in his *Emergence of the New South*, pp. 340–353. Another survey was written by Herbert J. Lahne, *The Cotton Mill Worker* (New York: Farrar & Rinehart, Inc., 1944). F. Ray Marshall's *Labor in the South*, mentioned earlier, provided a broad view of the CIO organizing effort in the South during the 1930s. Studies of the Tennessee Valley Authority differed as to its economic impact on the poor. The most useful studies for the post-1932 period were: C. Herman Pritchett, *The Tennessee Valley Authority: A Study in Public Administration* (Chapel Hill: The University of North Carolina Press, 1943); Philip Selznick, *TVA and the Grass Roots: A Study in the Sociology of Formal Organization* (Berkeley: University of California Press, 1949); and Norman I. Wengert, *Valley of Tomorrow: The TVA and Agriculture*, University of Tennessee Record *Extension Series*, XXVIII, No. 1, 1952. An unpublished manuscript by Edward N. Akin, " 'Mr. Donald's Help': The Birmingham Village of Avondale Mills

During the Great Depression," April, 1978, provides brief biographies of some of the mill workers.

A classic survey of Southern politics provided many insights: V. O. Key, Jr., *Southern Politics in State and Nation* (New York: Alfred A. Knopf, Inc., 1949). Of the many biographies of 1930s politicians, none addresses the issue of class division so well as T. Harry Williams, *Huey Long* (New York: Alfred A. Knopf, 1969).

For definitions of the Agrarian argument see their manifesto *I'll Take My Stand* (New York: Harper and Brothers Publishers, 1930). For interpretation see Virginia J. Rock, "The Making and Meaning of *I'll Take My Stand:* A Study of Utopian-Conservatism, 1925–1939," (Ph.D. dissertation, University of Minnesota, 1961). Many essays also proved helpful: Thomas J. Pressly, "Agrarianism: An Autopsy," *Sewanee Review,* XLIX (April-June, 1941), 145–163; Richard M. Weaver, "Agrarianism in Exile," *Sewanee Review,* LVIII (October-December, 1950), 586–606. One of the most negative criticisms was authored by James L. McDonald, "Reactionary Rebels: Agrarians in Defense of the South," *The Midwest Quarterly,* X (January, 1969), 155–172. A more affirmative treatment was written by Edward Shapiro, "The Southern Agrarians and the Tennessee Valley Authority," *American Quarterly,* XXII (Winter, 1970), 791–806. For the emergence of poor-white class consciousness during the 1930s see: C. Vann Woodward, "Hillbilly Realism," *The Southern Review,* IV (Spring, 1939), 676–681; Donald Davidson, "The Class Approach to Southern Problems," *The Southern Review,* V (Autumn, 1939), 261–272; and Monroe N. Work, "Problems of Adjustment of Race and Class in the South," *Social Forces,* XVI (October, 1937), 108–117.

The regionalist approach to Southern problems was best summarized in Howard W. Odum's massive *Southern Regions of the United States* (Chapel Hill: University of North Carolina Press, 1936). Odum created the journal *Social Forces* in 1922 to serve as a forum for his ideas and those of his colleagues and students. Useful articles for this chapter were: Howard Odum, "The Way of the South," *Social Forces,* XXIII (March, 1945), 258–268; no author, "Toward Regional Documentation," *Social Forces,* XXIII (March, 1945), 302–330. The March, 1945, issue of *Social Forces* carried the theme "In Search of the Regional Balance of America," and is an excellent statement of regionalist philosophy. Another useful source was Dewey W. Grantham, Jr., "The Regional Imagination: Social Scientists and the American South," *The Journal of Southern History,* XXXIV (February, 1968), 3–32. A somewhat presumptuous treatment of regionalism that criticized it for insufficient focus on economics was written by John Friedmann, "Poor Regions and Poor Nations: Perspectives on the Problem of Appalachia," *Southern Economic Journal,* XXXII (April, 1966), 465–473.

Of all the Southern writers who dealt with the South's poor whites during the 1930s, none is more moving than James Agee. His *Let Us Now Praise Famous Men* (New York: Houghton Mifflin Company, 1941; photographs by Walker Evans) only recently has received the attention it has deserved. I was greatly assisted by numerous essays on its author: Kenneth Seib, *James Agee: Promise and Fulfillment* (Pittsburgh: University of Pittsburgh Press, 1968); Robert Fitzgerald, "A Memoir," in *The Collected Short Prose of James Agee* (Boston: Houghton Mifflin, 1968); Alan Holder, "Encounter in Alabama: Agee and the Tenant Farmer," *The Virginia Quarterly Review,* XLII (Spring, 1966), 189–206. An excellent brief biography by Kerry W. Buckley was entitled "James Agee: The Early Years," 1972, unpublished manuscript in author's possession.

Better-known novelists who contributed to the popular image of Southern poor whites were discussed by Sylvia Jenkins Cook in a 1973 doctoral dissertation at the University of Michigan entitled "The Literary Treatment of the Southern Poor White in the 1930's." This work was published three years later under the title *From Tobacco Road to Route 66: The Southern Poor White in Fiction* (Chapel Hill: University of North Carolina Press, 1976). Audrey S. McIlwaine's work, described earlier, also was useful. Although Erskine Caldwell perpetuated many stereotypes about poor white degeneracy, he also coauthored with Margaret Bourke-White a sympathetic pictorial essay, *You Have Seen Their Faces* (New York: Viking Press, 1937).

For perspectives on religion and poor whites during the 1930s, I relied on works cited earlier and especially on Liston Pope's seminal, *Millhands and Preachers: A Study of Gastonia* (New Haven: Yale University Press, 1942); and Frank D. Alexander's "Religion in a Rural Community of the South," *American Sociological Review,* VI (April, 1941), 241–251. Edmund deS. Brunner's *Church Life in the Rural South* (New York: George H. Doran Co., 1923), provides valuable survey materials on a seventy county area of the South, with more detailed information on six of the counties.

Once again I relied on oral history for a more personal perspective on these events. Mrs. Kathleen Knight of Guin, Alabama, sharecropped with her family in both north Alabama and in the Mississippi Delta: Samford University Oral History Project with Mrs. Kathleen Knight at Guin, Alabama, January 23, 1975. Carl Forrester was one of the white tenants who received assistance from the Farm Security Administration: Samford University Oral History Project with Carl Forrester in Houston County, Alabama, January 18, 1975. Lillie Mae (Flynt) Beason grew up in the family of an Alabama sharecropper and is an unusually articulate interviewee: Samford University Oral History Project with Lillie Mae (Flynt) Beason in Steele, Alabama, January 3, 1976.

5. *Southern Poverty Forgotten and Discovered—Again*

The dramatic switch from sociological to economic interpretation of the "problem South" came after World War II. Sociologists remained important in the debate, but economic considerations figured larger even in their work. For useful examples, see: Rupert B. Vance and Nadia Danilevsky, *All These People: The Nation's Human Resources in the South* (Chapel Hill: The University of North Carolina Press, 1945); Selz C. Mayo, "Social Change, Social Movements and the Disappearing Sectional South," *Social Forces,* XLIII (October, 1964), 1–10; Lewis C. Copeland and W. K. McPherson, "Industrial Trends in the Tennessee Valley," *Social Forces,* XXIV (March, 1946), 273–283. George B. Tindall has offered a persuasive analysis of the transition from a sociological to an economic interpretation of the South: "The 'Colonial Economy' and the Growth Psychology: The South in the 1930's," *The South Atlantic Quarterly,* LXIV (Autumn, 1965), 465–477.

One of the most controversial articles by an economist was authored by William H. Nicholls. He maintained that the South could not at the same time continue its agrarian values and enjoy the fruits of industrial "progress." In fairness to Nicholls, he wrote his essay in 1960 to counter a bitter defense of segregation (one of the agrarian "values") and as a plea for racial moderation as a requisite of economic development: "Southern Tradition and Regional Economic Progress," *The Southern Economic Journal,* XXVI (January, 1960), 187–198. Nicholls's book *Southern Tradition and Regional Progress* (Chapel Hill: University of North Carolina Press, 1960), further developed the theme. His article, "The South as a Developing Area," *The Journal of Politics,* XXVI (February, 1964), 22–40, provided a useful overview of economic trends. Regional economic growth was also the major focus of Lawrence Logan Durisch, "Southern Regional Planning and Development," *The Journal of Politics,* XXVI (February, 1964), 41–59.

The October, 1946, issue of *Monthly Labor Review* (volume LXIII), was part of a series on regional labor problems. This issue contained seven articles on the AFL and CIO. Unfortunately, the study did not distinguish by race in its statistics. Nevertheless, I found two essays to be particularly useful: Sophia C. Mendelsohn and Lester M. Pearlman, "Labor Supply in the South," 484–494, and Solomon Shapiro, "Income in the South," 495–510.

The March, 1968, issue of *Monthly Labor Review* (volume XCI) returned to the region, this time with twice as many articles and with statistical data arranged by race. See particularly Ray Marshall, "The Development of Organized Labor," 65–73, which summarized his book, *Labor in the South;* and William J. Stober, "Employment and Economic Growth: Southeast," 16–23.

Southern manufacturing growth was the topic of a considerable body of literature about industrial patterns, urbanization, labor supply, and income. For industrial growth see: Martin A. Garrett, Jr., "Growth in Manufacturing in the South, 1947–1958: A Study in Regional Industrial Development," *The Southern Economic Journal*, XXXIV (January, 1968), 352–364; Stephen McDonald, "On the South's Recent Economic Development," *The Southern Economic Journal*, XXVIII (July, 1961), 30–40; Charles G. Leathers, "Alabama's Relative State and Local Tax Burden," *Journal of the Alabama Academy of Science*, XLI (October, 1970), 240–245; B. U. Ratchford, "Patterns of Economic Development," *The Southern Economic Journal*, XX (January, 1954), 217–230.

Agricultural economics took preeminence over discussion of tenancy during the 1940s and '50s. For examples, see: J. Allan Tower, "Cotton Change in Alabama, 1879–1946," *Economic Geography*, XXVI (January, 1950), 6–28; Franklin C. Erickson, "The Broken Cotton Belt," *Economic Geography*, XXIV (October, 1948), 263–268; Vernon W. Ruttan, "Farm and Non-Farm Employment Opportunities for Low Income Farm Families," *Phylon*, XX (Autumn, 1959), 248–255.

A few academicians continued to explore the problems of tenancy, and many others joined them in the 1960s and 1970s. For an excellent overview, see Lee G. Burchinal and Hilda Siff of the Department of Health, Education, and Welfare: "Rural Poverty," *Journal of Marriage and the Family*, XXVI (November, 1964), 399–405. Four studies focused on individuals, regions, or aspects of rural life: Dorothy Dickins, "Food Patterns of White and Negro Families, 1936–1948," *Social Forces*, XXVII (May, 1949), 425–430, was a comparative study done on the Mississippi Delta; sociologists Mozell C. Hill and Bevode C. McCall, "Social Stratification in 'Georgia Town,'" *American Sociological Review*, XV (December, 1950), 721–729, examined black-white poverty in a south Georgia county seat in 1949; Hodding Carter's "The South's Forgotten Man," *The Saturday Evening Post*, CCXXII (August 20, 1949), 25, 88, is a brief, unforgettable essay on a poor white Mississippian. Margaret Pace Farmer focused on a major Alabama cotton-producing county and the changes that occurred between 1910 and 1964: "Furnishing Merchants and Sharecroppers in Pike County, Alabama," *The Alabama Review*, XXIII (April, 1970), 143–151. The most useful source for this topic, however, was a doctoral dissertation in economics at the New School for Social Research: Arthur M. Ford, "Political Economics of Rural Poverty in the South," 1973.

The out-migration that resulted from high birth rates and technological change will be discussed more fully in the chapter on Appalachia. However, two sources were used in this chapter: Selz C. Mayo and C. Horace Hamilton, "Current Population Trends in the South," *Social Forces*, LXII (October, 1963), 77–78; and Rashi Fein, "Educational Patterns in Southern Migration," *The Southern Economic Journal*, XXXII (July, 1965), 106–124.

The creation of a new industrial class is the major topic of Rudolf Heberle's "The Changing Social Stratification of the South," *Social Forces*, XXXVIII (October, 1959), 42–50. For the effect of political activity on industrial wages, see: John M. Peterson, "Employment Effects of Minimum Wages, 1938–1950," *The Journal of Political Economy*, LXV (October, 1957), 412–430; Lloyd Saville, "Earnings of Skilled and Unskilled Workers in New England and the South," *The Journal of Political Economy*, LXII (October, 1954), 390–405; Paul A. Brinker, "The South: Stagnation or Progress," *The American Federationist*, LXIX (July, 1962), 16–18. Organizing efforts in the 1940s by both the CIO and the AFL are the central themes in Frank T. de Vyver, "Union Fratricide: The Textile Workers Split," *The South Atlantic Quarterly*, LXIII (Summer, 1964), 363–384. A prounion view is found in J. L. Rhodes, "Dixie is Jumping," *The American Federationist*, LIX (February, 1952), 227. A judicious analysis of "Operation Dixie," its failure, and the barriers to unionism in the South was presented by F. Ray Marshall, "Impediments to Labor Union Organization in the South," *The South Atlantic Quarterly*, LVII (Autumn, 1958), 409–418. Marshall particularly was perceptive in his comprehension that evangelicalism served as both hindrance and help for unionism. For one exceptional Alabama Baptist minister who worked to help impoverished farmers and workers, see Samford University Oral History Project with Rev. Charles R. Bell, Jr., at Anniston, Alabama, August 28, 1972.

Few topics have been treated more thoroughly than Southern poverty in the 1960s. Michael Harrington's book *The Other America: Poverty in the United States* (New York: Macmillan, 1962) was widely credited with initiating a series of federal programs that are generally lumped together as the "poverty program." Dwight MacDonald's essay in *The New Yorker*, XXXVIII (January 19, 1963), 82+, entitled "Our Invisible Poor" was one of the most articulate summaries. Ben B. Seligman penned a similar essay, "American Poverty: Rural and Urban," *Current History*, LV (October, 1968), 193–198. Catherine Chilman and Marvin B. Sussman of the U. S. Department of Health, Education, and Welfare and Western Reserve University elaborated statistically in their article "Poverty in the United States in the Mid-Sixties," *Journal of Marriage and the Family*, XXVI (November, 1964), 391–395. The special issue for March, 1968, of *Monthly Labor Review* (volume XCI) contained several valuable articles: Vernon M. Biggs, Jr., "Manpower Programs and Regional Development," 55–61; Helen H. Lamale and Thomas J. Lanahan, Jr., "Income and Levels of Living," 90–96; H. M. Douty, "Wage Differentials: Forces and Counterforces," 74–81. Two statistical studies by the Southern Regional Council provided important information: Gretchen MacLachlan, *The Other Twenty Percent: A Statistical Analysis of Poverty in the South* (Atlanta: Southern Regional Council, 1974); *Health Care in the South: A Statistical Profile* (Atlanta: Southern Regional Council, 1974). Both of these documented the persistence of poverty despite all the remedial federal legislation of the 1960s. The same conclusion emerged from the Report of the President's Commission on Income Maintenance Programs: *Poverty Amid Plenty: The American Paradox* (Washington: U.S. Government Printing Office, 1969). One of the most hopeful essays discussed private industry's development in the rural South: Thomas Edward Till, "Rural Industrialization and Southern Rural Poverty: Patterns of Labor Demand in Southern Nonmetropolitan Labor Markets and Their Impact on the Poor, 1959–1969," unpublished Ph.D. dissertation in economics, University of Texas at Austin, 1972.

Race was a factor in poor white reaction to various federal programs dealing with poverty. One body of literature concluded that white indigents avoided programs that were identified with civil rights or in which substantial numbers of blacks participated. A sample follows: Melvin M. Tumin, "Readiness and Resistance to Desegregation: A Social Portrait of the Hard Core," *Social Forces*, XXXVI (December, 1957), 256–263 (a case study of Guilford County, North Carolina); Earl Black and Merle Black, "The Wallace Vote in Alabama: A Multiple Regression Analysis," *The Journal of Politics*, XXXV (August, 1973), 730–736; James K. Batten, "A Cold Shoulder For the Poverty Program," *The Reporter*, XXXVIII (May 30, 1968), 26–28 (focusing on Craven County, North Carolina); Harry Golden, "Poor Whites in Rural North Carolina," *The Nation*, CCVI (May 20, 1968), 668; James D. Cowhig and Calvin L. Beale, "Relative

Socio-economic Status of Southern Whites and Nonwhites, 1950–1960,"
Southwestern Social Science Quarterly, XLV (September, 1964), 113–
124; Robert Dare, "Involvement of the Poor in Atlanta," *Phylon*, XXXI
(Summer, 1970), 114–128; C. Arnold Anderson, "Inequalities in Schooling in the South," *The American Journal of Sociology*, LX (May, 1955),
547–561. Numan V. Bartley and Hugh D. Graham argued that the political
reaction of poor whites to the civil rights movement destroyed the old New
Deal coalition of blacks and poor whites: *Southern Politics and the Second
Reconstruction* (Baltimore: The Johns Hopkins University Press, 1975).

Other authors emphasized the common problems faced by the poor of
both races, and concluded that this commonality has caused them to work
together to resolve mutual problems: James W. Prothro, Ernest Q. Campbell, and Charles M. Grigg, "Two-Party Voting in the South: Class vs.
Party Identification," *The American Political Science Review*, LII (March,
1958), 131–139; Anthony M. Orum and Edward W. McCranie, "Class,
Tradition, and Partisan Alignments in a Southern Urban Electorate," *The
Journal of Politics*, XXXII (February, 1970), 156–176. Two doctoral dis-
sertations elaborated the same opinion. Political scientist David H. Tabb
was surprised to find stronger class feelings than racial animosities among
poor whites in Durham, North Carolina, in 1966: "Attitudes Toward Economic Equality in the South: A Study of the Political Ideology of the
Poor," unpublished Ph.D. dissertation in political science, University of
North Carolina at Chapel Hill, 1969. Economist Lee S. Balliet used Southern history as well as contemporary community organization in support of
his thesis that biracial economic cooperation was consistent with the regional past and with current political realities: "Anglo Poverty in the
Rural South," unpublished Ph.D. dissertation in economics, University of
Texas at Austin, 1974. Specific examples of biracial economic and political
activity can be found in Balliet's work and in two additional essays: Peter
Barnes, "Pulpwood Peonage," *The New Republic*, CLXVI (March 18,
1972), 15–17; Rex Herdesty, "The New Mississippi," *The American Federationist*, LXXVIII (July, 1971), 12–18. As in earlier chapters, the
work of Robert Coles furnished critical perspectives, especially his insight
into the subdued but frustrating anger that lurked within apparently placid
and fatalistic poor folk. Of his many works, the most useful for this point
is his *Migrants, Sharecroppers, Mountaineers* (Boston: Little, Brown and
Co., 1971).

Paul Hemphill's *The Good Old Boys* (New York: Anchor Press, 1975)
contained valuable impressions of poor-white cultural survivals, such as
the popularity of wrestling, stock car racing, football, and baseball.

A diverse literature exists on the fascinating subject of country music.

Whether in its original style ("Doc" Watson on guitar or "Grandpa" Jones on five-string banjo) or its recent popularizations ("bluegrass," "country-western," the "Nashville Sound"), there is adequate comment. In addition to Guy and Candie Carawan, *Voices From the Mountains* (New York: Alfred A. Knopf, 1975), and Archie Green, *Only A Miner: Studies in Recorded Coal-Mining Songs,* mentioned earlier, I learned from my more musically inclined Samford history colleague, James S. Brown (for information on guitar, dulcimer, five-string banjo), and many written sources: C. P. Heaton, "The 5-String Banjo in North Carolina," *Southern Folklore Quarterly,* XXV (December, 1961), 226–237; Frye Gaillard, "Sour Notes at the Grand Ole Opry," *Southern Voices,* I (May/June, 1974), 42–50 (a superior analysis of the cultural roots of the Opry phenomenon); Paul Hendrickson, "Goodbye to all that, y'all," *New Times* (April 19, 1974), 54–58. In addition, the interested student should place himself before a stereo or live "fiddle festival" as frequently as possible, a form of research which was the most enjoyable part of preparing this manuscript.

Folk religion holds a special fascination for me, but I will make no attempt to list the lengthy scholarly bibliography in the sociology of religion or Southern evangelicalism. My own view is that Southern evangelicals were both more realistic and involved with society than most scholars have concluded. Also, their otherworldliness needs to be understood for the value and meaning it provided them, and less for the lack of meaning it may hold for a more secular society: Robert Coles, "God and the Rural Poor," *Psychology Today,* V (January, 1972), 31–41; David Edwin Harrell, Jr., *White Sects and Black Men in the Recent South* (Nashville: Vanderbilt University Press, 1971), and his *All Things Are Possible: The Healing and Charismatic Revivals in Modern America* (Bloomington: Indiana University Press, 1975), provided a refreshingly different view of Pentecostalism; Will D. Campbell and James Y. Holloway (editors), *The Failure and the Hope* (Grand Rapids: Eerdmans, 1972). More traditional sources utilized for the discussion of Southern religion were: Catherine T. Harris, "Patterns of Religious and Political Involvement: Theoretical Implications from Max Weber," *The Journal of the Alabama Academy of Science,* XLIII (January, 1972), 32–40; George L. Maddox and Joseph H. Fichter, "Religion and Social Change in the South," *The Journal of Social Issues,* XXII (January, 1966), 44–58.

6. *Appalachian Spring—And Winter*

Primary credit for this chapter, especially its theoretical perspective, really belongs to the people of Appalachia. During a decade of camping among, fishing with, and talking to such folk, my interpretation emerged. I owe some of them such a large debt that I must acknowledge it more specifically. Chancellor Joseph C. Smiddy of Clinch Valley College in Wise, Virginia, is a biologist by training, but an advocate of Appalachian culture by avocation. He introduced me to the intricacies of mountain music, the five-string banjo, dulcimer, and guitar. More importantly, Smiddy's collection of ballad manuscripts, especially from the 1930s depression era, is a major contribution to Appalachian scholarship. Furthermore, Chancellor Smiddy introduced me to one of his faculty members, Sociology Professor Helen Lewis, whose work confirmed my own prejudices about mountain culture. I strongly recommend her work, much of which is available only in manuscript form. A sample follows: "The Colonialism Model: The Appalachian Case," coauthored by Edward Knipe; "Occupational Roles and Family Roles: A Study of Coal Mining Families in the Southern Appalachians," unpublished Ph.D. dissertation in sociology, University of Kentucky, 1970; and three other unpublished manuscripts by Professor Lewis: "Medicos and Mountaineers: The Meeting of Two Cultures," 1971; "The Subcultures of the Southern Appalachians: Their Origins and Boundary Maintenance," 1967; "Family, Religion and Colonialism in Central Appalachia or Bury My Rifle at Big Stone Gap," coauthored by Sue Easterling Kobak and Linda Johnson, 1972.

Scattered throughout this chapter are references to a series of Samford University Oral History Projects that have been of assistance in providing the perspective that dominates the chapter: Mary Thompson's Oral History Project with Jim Hammitte at Hamilton, Alabama, November 23, 1974; my own projects with retired coal miners Lloyd Vick Minor, Pennington Gap, Virginia, August 20, 1974; L. F. Minor, Big Stone Gap, Virginia, August 20, 1974; Fred Gaddis and M. C. Sizemore of Stonega, Virginia, August 21, 1974; Glen G. Carter, Dryden, Virginia, August 21, 1974; and with Chancellor Joseph C. Smiddy, Wise, Virginia, August 23, 1974.

The nature of Appalachian subculture is the topic of many studies. For the "subculture of poverty" approach, see John F. Bauman, "The Scope of the Poverty Program," *Current History,* LXI (November, 1971), 284; Richard A. Ball, "A Poverty Case: The Analgesic Subculture of the Southern Appalachians," *American Sociological Review,* XXXIII (December, 1968), 885–894. For more sympathetic portraits of mountain character, but still dominated by references to fatalism, familism, fundamentalism, and traditionalism, see: *The Southern Appalachian Region: A Survey* (Lexington: University of Kentucky Press, 1962), a superb anthology edited by Thomas R. Ford, who was the major professor of Helen Lewis; Harry M. Caudill, *Night Comes to the Cumberlands: A Biography of a Depressed*

Area (Boston: Little, Brown and Company, 1962), a shattering, impressionistic study by a Whitesburg, Kentucky, lawyer-writer; Cratis D. Williams, "Who Are the Southern Mountaineers?" *Appalachian Journal*, I (Autumn, 1972), 48–57; Robert Coles, "Farewell to Appalachia," *Appalachian Journal* I (Autumn, 1972), 22–24; and W. K. McNeil, "The Eastern Kentucky Mountaineer: An External and Internal View of History," *Mid-South Folklore*, I (Summer, 1973), 35–54 (this article provided excellent insight into the evolution of the hillbilly stereotype and took issue with Caudill's notion that most Appalachian people descended from orphans and outlaws, or shiftless, unskilled, illiterate folk).

Despite the labor violence of Harlan County, Kentucky, during the 1930s, a slim bibliography confronts the researcher. Perhaps the most useful sources I found were: John W. Hevener, "New Deal Labor Policies in Harlan County, Kentucky, 1933–1939," an unpublished manuscript delivered at the Association of Southern Labor Historians meeting in Louisville, Kentucky, in 1970; Tony Bubka, "The Harlan County Coal Strike of 1931," *Labor History*, XI (Winter, 1970), 41–57; and Harry M. Caudill, "The Permanent Poor: The Lesson of Eastern Kentucky," *The Atlantic*, CCXIII (June, 1964), 49–53. I learned almost as much, however, from the songs of Harlan County musicians; Archie Green's *Only A Miner* is an important source for this entire chapter.

Appalachian migration has attracted much greater interest than labor unrest, and the starting place for research is Robert Coles, *The South Goes North* (Boston: Little, Brown, 1971). An extensive body of research amplified Coles' insights: Thomas R. Ford and Gordon F. DeGong, "The Decline of Fertility in the Southern Appalachian Mountain Region," *Social Forces*, XLII (October, 1963), 89–96; Terry G. Jordan, "The Texan Appalachian," *Annals of the Association of American Geographers*, LX (September, 1960), 409–427, an excellent study of nineteenth-century Appalachian migration to the Texas hill country and the persistence there of mountain culture; Woodrow R. Clevinger, "Southern Appalachian Highlanders in Western Washington," *The Pacific Northwest Quarterly*, XXXIII (January, 1942), 3–25, which does the same for the Pacific slopes as Jordan's essay does for Texas. David E. Kaun, "Wage Adjustments in the Appalachian States," *The Southern Economic Journal*, XXXII (July, 1965), 73–102, examined the economic and social impact of the migration of poor whites to Northern cities. The entire issue for April-June, 1970, of the *Journal of American Folklore* (volume LXXXIII) was devoted to "The Urban Experience and Folk Tradition" and included such disparate topics as the relationship of country-western music to the urban hillbilly, the process of cultural stripping and reintegration, and folk medicine. The most valuable essay was Ellen J. Stekert, "Focus for Conflict: Southern Mountain Medical Beliefs in Detroit," 115–148. An excellent sample of the popular stereotyping of hillbillies as antisocial degenerates can be found in Albert N. Votaw, "The Hillbillies Invade Chicago," *Harper's Magazine,* CCXVI (February, 1958), 64–67.

The "discovery" of Appalachian poverty also inspired a wealth of literature, both academic and popular. The most useful studies were the President's Appalachian Regional Commission, *Appalachia,* 1964, and the annual summaries of projects and programs by the Regional Commission: *The Appalachian Regional Commission, Annual Report,* by years. An early proposal for solving technical problems in determining the extent of Appalachian poverty was Herman P. Miller, "Statistical Gaps in the War on Poverty," *Monthly Labor Review,* LXXXVII (August, 1964), 887–888. Numerous articles appeared in the 1960s focusing on specific counties: "Mountains of Poverty," *The Economist,* CXCI (April 25, 1959), 333–344, dealt with Leslie County, Kentucky; Reese Cleghorn, "Appalachia—Poverty, Beauty and Poverty," *The New York Times Magazine,* April 25, 1965, p. 12, considered Dawson County, Georgia; Margaret Anderson, "Education in Appalachia: Past Failures and Future Prospects," *Journal of Marriage and the Family,* XXVI (November, 1964), 443–446.

Popular treatments are interesting, if only for photographs and stereotypes, and sometimes convey significant insights: Marjorie Hunter, "The Mountains of Poverty," *The New York Times Magazine,* May 17, 1964, pp. 12–13; "Portrait of An Underdeveloped Country," *Look,* XXVI (December 4, 1962), 25–33; "The Valley of Poverty," *Life,* LVI (January 31, 1964), 54–65; "New Way to Beat Poverty: the Plan for Appalachia," *U.S. News and World Report,* LIX (September 27, 1965), 68–70; "Human Erosion," *Fortune,* LXXVIII (August, 1968), 74; "Poverty in Appalachia: A Report After Five Years of Aid," *U.S. News and World Report,* LXV (July 29, 1968), 50–53.

Following the exploration of the problem, the literature leaned more heavily toward proposed solutions. The best chronological summary of various federal programs affecting poor whites was James E. Anderson's "Poverty, Unemployment, and Economic Development: The Search for a National Antipoverty Policy," *The Journal of Politics,* XXIX (February, 1967), 70–93. John Friedmann makes some debatable comparisons in an otherwise useful article, "Poor Regions and Poor Nations: Perspectives on the Problem of Appalachia," *The Southern Economic Journal,* XXXII (April, 1966), 465–473. One of the most impressive analyses was done by the President's National Advisory Committee on Rural Poverty: *The People Left Behind,* 1967. Geographer Truman A. Hartshorn criticized the Appalachian program and favored concentrating federal aid toward the development of intermediate-sized Appalachian cities: "The Spatial Structure of Socioeconomic Development in the Southeast, 1950–1960," *The Geographical Review,* LXI (April, 1971), 265–283. Carl W. Hale's essay, "Factors Inhibiting Appalachian Regional Development: West Virginia, a Case Study," *American Journal of Economics and Sociology,* XXX (April, 1971), 133–158, concentrated on poor transportation and rural political dominance. George L. Hicks, *Appalachian Valley* (New York: Holt, Rinehart and Winston, 1976), examined why he believed the Appalachian poverty program failed.

Discussions of the Appalachian society included Harry W. Ernst and Charles H. Drake, "Poor, Proud and Primitive," *The Nation,* CLXXXVIII (May 30, 1959), 490–493, which was filled with cultural assumptions of superiority to Appalachian folkways. The same was true of Roman B. Aquizap and Ernest A. Vargas, "Technology, Power and Socialization in Appalachia," *Social Casework,* LI (March, 1970), 131–139, who argued the dubious conclusion that the region's salvation depended upon replacing "stubbornness and passive aggression" with aggressive social behavior and striving against the system. Mary W. Wright, "Public Assistance in the Appalachian South," *Journal of Marriage and the Family,* XXVI (November, 1964), 406–409, was a sensitive essay on the welfare bureaucracy which emasculated and humiliated even as it provided critical assistance. Two superior essays challenged the initial assumptions of the Appalachian Regional Development program, arguing that the priority given highway construction ignored the decay of human resources and the immediate lack of jobs. Both articles were extremely useful: Ben B. Seligman, "American Poverty: Rural and Urban," *Current History,* LV (October, 1968), 193–198; "Appalachia As Symbol," *The Nation,* CC (February 22, 1965), 182.

For contemporary labor unrest in Appalachia, I utilized: Emil Malizia, "Economic Imperialism: An Interpretation of Appalachian Underdevelopment," *Appalachian Journal,* I (Spring, 1973), 130–137; James Lieber, "Bloody Harlan Strikes Again," *New Times* (April 19, 1974), pp. 22–27; Lawrence Wright, "Back to Bloody Harlan," *Southern Voices,* I (May/June, 1974), 53–55; Reese Cleghorn, "Appalachia—Poverty, Beauty And Poverty," *The New York Times Magazine,* April 25, 1965, p. 12. Except for the *New York Times Magazine* these articles appeared in little-known journals of limited circulation. This, perhaps, supports my basic argument that discovering what it was like to be a coal miner, to see the economics of energy from his very personal reference point, is a subjective but necessary exercise. I particularly recommend the short-lived *Southern Voices.*

While it lasted, it published more important and provocative literature on Southern poor whites than any journal in America. Two more accessible recent publications were more dramatic than substantive; yet both came at Appalachia from the perspective of the common folk: Kathy Kahn, *Hillbilly Women* (New York: Avon Books, 1972); and Guy and Candie Carawan, *Voices From the Mountains*, cited earlier. A new journal published by the Institute for Southern Studies, *Southern Exposure*, holds promise of filling the void left by the demise of *Southern Voices*.

The craft revival was essential to the self-consciousness of mountain people. I am indebted to a Samford University coed, Lee Hazlegrove, for a superior essay on "The Revival of Weaving, Southern Highlands, 1900–1935," unpublished manuscript, 1974, especially for explaining the roles of Berea College and mountain missionary Louisa Goodrich. Standard works on this subject are John C. Campbell, *The Southern Highlander and His Homeland* (Chapel Hill: University of North Carolina Press, 1921); Allen H. Eaton, *Handicrafts of the Southern Highlands* (New York: Russell Sage Foundation, 1937). The Dover edition of this classic, published in 1973, contained important introductory essays by Ralph Rinzler and Rayna Green. A contemporary but more personal and impressionistic rediscovery of Alabama folk culture was Carl Carmer's *Stars Fell On Alabama* (New York: Blue Ribbon Books, Inc., 1934). An essential but little-known article was based on a survey taken in 1934 by Bertha M. Nienburg of the Women's Bureau of the Department of Labor. The research was published by the U. S. Department of Labor as "Potential Earning Power of Southern Mountaineer Handicraft," Bulletin No. 128, 1935. A more accessible summary of the research appeared under the title "Earnings of Handicraft Workers in Southern Mountain Regions," *Monthly Labor Review*, XLI (July, 1935), 146–149.

For the survival of folk beliefs, I relied upon John Q. Anderson, "Popular Beliefs in Texas, Louisiana, and Arkansas," *Southern Folklore Quarterly*, XXXII (September, 1968), 304–319; William Lynwood Montell, *Ghosts Along the Cumberland* (Knoxville: University of Tennessee Press, 1975); Richard Chase, *The Jack Tales* (Boston: Houghton Mifflin, 1943).

Two essays from James Y. Holloway's *The Failure and the Hope*, cited earlier, are essential reading in order to understand Appalachian culture: Will D. Campbell, "Footwashing or the New Hermeneutic," and James G. Barnscome's "Annihilating the Hillbilly: The Appalachians' Struggle with America's Institutions."

On the snake-handling cult, there are two excellent academic articles: Ellen Stekert, "The Snake-Handling Sect of Harlan County, Kentucky: Its Influence on Folk Tradition," *Southern Folklore Quarterly*, XXVII

(December, 1963), 316–322; Steven M. Kane, "Holy Ghost People: The Snake-Handlers of Southern Appalachia," *Appalachian Journal,* I (Spring, 1974), 255–262. One of the most gripping sources, however, was a film of such a service that allowed the people to speak for themselves: "They Shall Take Up Serpents," produced by East Tennessee State University in conjunction with the Tennessee Arts Commission, a seventeen-minute film made in 1972.

Four articles allowed mountain people to speak directly, in one way or another, and it is the method I have chosen to end this book: Jack E. Weller "Is There a Future for Yesterday's People?" *The Saturday Review of Literature,* XLVIII (October 16, 1965), 33–36; Robert H. Woody, "Cataloochee Homecoming," *The South Atlantic Quarterly,* XLIX (January, 1950), 8–17; "Ballads and Rhymes from Kentucky," *Appalachian Heritage,* II (Winter, 1974), 19–26; Loyal Jones, "What I Would Like To See Happen To Our Land And People," *Appalachian Heritage,* I (Summer, 1973), 21–22.

Notes

Chapter One

1. Governmental surveys unfortunately adopted a shifting definition of the South that required specific listing of the states, a practice which will be followed in discussions of conditions in the twentieth century. The fluctuating meaning of both poverty and the South occurred within certain periods of time; therefore, a chronological pattern must be followed except for Appalachia, whose unique historical isolation following the Civil War created a way of life so distinctive as to require separate attention. The first chapter will explore the social structure and economic organization of antebellum poor whites, and the following chapter will examine their culture and values during the same era.

2. Quoted in Elizabeth Wisner, *Social Welfare in the South: From Colonial Times to World War I* (Baton Rouge: Louisiana State University Press, 1970), pp. 39–40.

3. Quoted in John B. Boles, *The Great Revival, 1787–1805: The Origins of the Southern Evangelical Mind* (Lexington: University of Kentucky Press, 1972), pp. 118–119.

Chapter Two

1. Arnold J. Toynbee, *A Study of History* (London: Oxford University Press, 1947), vol. I, p. 149.

2. Quoted in William Ferris, "Don't Throw It Away," *Yale Alumni Magazine*, 37 (March, 1974), 22.

3. Augustus Baldwin Longstreet, *Georgia Scenes* (Augusta, Ga., 1840 edition), pp. 54–55.

4. Quoted in James T. Pearce, "Folk Tales of the Southern Poor-

White, 1820–1860," *Journal of American Folklore,* 63 (October-December, 1950), 401.

5. Cecil Sharp, comp., and Maud Karpeles, ed., *English Folk Songs from the Southern Appalachians* (London: Oxford University Press; 1952 edition), vol. I, pp. 230–231.

Chapter Three

1. Samford University Oral History Project with Jessie Thrasher, at McCalla, Alabama, November 12, 1974.

2. Quoted on page 193, Maybelle Coleman, "Poverty and Poor Relief in the Plantation Society of South Carolina: A Study in the Sociology of a Social Problem," Ph.D. dissertation, Duke University, 1943.

3. Samford University Oral History Project with Mrs. L. A. House, at Sylacauga, Alabama, July 10, 1974.

4. Samford University Oral History Project with Elmer Burton, in Walker County, Alabama, December 3, 1974.

5. Recorded by Vance Randolph, "Tales From Arkansas," *Southern Folklore Quarterly,* XIX (June, 1955), 130–131.

6. Ibid.

Chapter Four

1. Samford University Oral History Project with Mrs. Lillie Mae (Flynt) Beason at Steele, Alabama, January 3, 1976.

2. Unless otherwise specified, the South is defined as the eleven former Confederate states plus Oklahoma and Kentucky.

3. Samford University Oral History Project with Mrs. Kathleen Knight at Guin, Alabama, January 23, 1975.

4. Edward N. Akin, " 'Mr. Donald's Help:' The Birmingham Village of Avondale Mills During the Great Depression," April, 1978, unpublished manuscript.

5. Quoted in Edmund deS. Brunner, *Church Life in the Rural South,* George H. Doran, 1923, p. 21.

6. James Agee and Walker Evans, *Let Us Now Praise Famous Men,* Ballantine Book edition, 1973, pp. 129–130.

7. Quoted on pages 3 and 4, Paul Eric Mertz, " 'Economic Problem No. 1,' The New Deal and Southern Poverty," Ph.D. dissertation in history, University of Oklahoma, 1972.

8. Samford University Oral History Project with Carl Forrester in rural Houston County, Alabama, January 18, 1975.

9. Interview with H. L. Mitchell, April 21, 1972, Birmingham, Alabama.

Chapter Five

1. Jessie L. Thrift, "A Rebel for Christ," undated campaign brochure in author's possession. I made no changes in punctuation or grammar.

Chapter Six

1. Samford University Oral History Project with M. C. Sizemore at Stonega, Virginia, August 21, 1974.

2. Samford University Oral History Project with Jim Hammitte at Hamilton, Alabama, November 23, 1974.

3. Quoted in Helen Matthews Lewis, Linda Johnson, and Sue Easterling Kobak, "Family, Religion and Colonialism in Central Appalachia or Bury My Rifle at Big Stone Gap," unpublished manuscript read to American Anthropological Association, 1972, p. 11.

4. Quoted in Steven M. Kane's "Holy Ghost People: The Snake-Handlers of Southern Appalachia," *Appalachian Journal*, 1 (Spring, 1974), 255–262.

5. Quoted on page 390 of Archie Green, *Only A Miner: Studies In Recorded Coal-Mining Songs* (Urbana: University of Illinois Press, 1972).

6. Loyal Jones, "What I Would Like To See Happen To Our Land and People," *Appalachian Heritage*, 1 (Summer, 1973), 21–22.

Index